WORDS That Moved the World

HOW TO STUDY THE QUR'ĀN

Qazi Ashfaq Ahmad

THE ISLAMIC FOUNDATION

ISBN 0 86037 292 8 (PB)

Published by
The Islamic Foundation,
Markfield Conference Centre,
Ratby Lane, Markfield,
Leicester LE67 9SY,
United Kingdom
Tel: (01530) 244944, Fax: (01530) 244946
E-mail: i.foundation@islamic-foundation.org.uk
Web site: http://www.islamic-foundation.org.uk/islamfound

Quran House,
PO Box 30611,
Nairobi,
Kenya

PMB 3193,
Kano,
Nigeria

Cover Design by Imtiaze Ahmed Manjra

بِسْمِ اللَّهِ الرَّحْمَٰنِ الرَّحِيمِ

Contents

Acknowledgement 5

Preface 7

Introduction 11

Chapter One ***Bismillāhir Raḥmānir Raḥīm (In the name of Allah, Most Gracious, Most Merciful)*** 15

Chapter Two ***Revelation – The Word of God*** 23
- 2.1 The Absolute Truth 23
- 2.2 The Qur'ān Defines Itself 25
- 2.3 The Qur'ān Assigns Itself Other Names 31

Chapter Three ***Doctrines*** 45
- 3.1 Paradigm Shift from the Mundane to the Magnificent 45
- 3.2 The Purpose of the Qur'ān 47
- 3.3 *Tawḥīd* – The Oneness of Allah 51
- 3.4 *Ākhirah* – The Life Hereafter 59
- 3.5 The Achievement of the Qur'ān 71

Chapter Four ***Historical Perspective*** 75
- 4.1 The Purpose of Human Creation 75
- 4.2 The Purpose of the Creation of Rational Beings 84
- 4.3 The Purpose of Revelation 85

Chapter Five ***Prophethood*** 89
5.1 Muḥammad (peace be upon him) 89
5.2 Prophethood 92
5.3 The Man-Prophet 94
5.4 The Finality of Prophethood 95

Chapter Six ***The Message and the Messenger*** 97
6.1 The Absoluteness of Ethics 97
6.2 Muḥammad (peace be upon him) and the Qur'ān 98
6.3 Following the Ordinance of the Prophet (peace be upon him) 100
6.4 Manifestation of the Word of Allah 101

Chapter Seven ***Themes of the Qur'ān*** 103
7.1 Divine Lifestyle 103
7.2 Foundational Message 104
7.3 Self-Surrender to Allah 106
7.4 The Qur'ān and Consciousness of Allah 108

Chapter Eight ***The Book of Knowledge*** 111
8.1 A Unique Book 111
8.2 The Qur'ān and Science 113
8.3 Embryology 121

Chapter Nine ***Initial Study of the Qur'ān*** 125
9.1 The Importance of Reading and Understanding the Qur'ān 125
9.2 Primary Principles About the Qur'ān 127
9.3 Objectives of the Study 130
9.4 Comprehension of the Qur'ān 131
9.5 The Qur'ān and *Ṣalāt* 133

Glossary 135
Index 139

Acknowledgement

I commence this book with the time-honoured formula of introduction for the Holy Qur'ān. In so doing I dedicate this work to Almighty Allah, the Giver of the Divine Word of Al-Qur'ān.

I thank the Islamic Foundation, Leicester for their interest and support in publishing my work. The encouragement and help rendered by the Islamic Foundation for Education and Welfare (IFEW) in Australia is also acknowledged. Special thanks go to Sr. Shifa Mustafa, Queensland, Australia for checking the manuscript and giving valuable suggestions. My daughters Fauzia Siddiqui and Najia Khalil assisted me in collecting the material and reading the manuscript for further suggestions. I should also thank Jameela Ho for typing the manuscript in its initial stages. Last but not least, I owe a lot to my wife, living family and integrated family for their constant encouragement and patience demonstrated in hard times.

May Allah accept this humble venture and let it reach those who will benefit from it.

Wa mā 'alainā illal-balāgh

Preface

In 1930 I was born of a Muslim family, in India, a land of almost insurmountable tension between Hindus and Muslims. That I was Muslim was merely a fact of life, and I neither doubted, nor yet had knowledge enough to substantiate my belief in Islam. Even of this I was ignorant until one day I was questioned by a Hindu acquaintance. 'How much do you know of this Religion of yours, this Islam?', he queried. Dumbfounded, it was at that point that I realised that indeed I knew precious little regarding this most important aspect of my life.

Having graduated in Engineering I left this sphere of learning for almost five years, so that I could study Arabic and Islam. Would this mean the rejection of the Religion of my birth?

In search of a rational parameter, I was led to the Holy Qur'ān. It was during this study that I realised how infinitely miraculous is the plan of Almighty Allah, and how marvellous is His Guidance in the form of the Holy Qur'ān. Plunging into its ocean of Revelations and learning, I realised that I was a traveller who had not only lost my way, but had not even had the understanding to realise that this pathway had been there for me from birth. No longer was I a Muslim in name only, no longer a prey to ignorance bordering on hypocrisy, but, at last, making an effort to travel on the right path.

The Qur'ān is the embodiment of a harmonious blend of austerity and contentment. This harmonious integration is the distinctive mark of the Qur'ān. The Omniscient, Almighty God, revealed His intent through the last Messenger, in the form of the Qur'ān – the Ocean of Knowledge and Wisdom. Man can give meaning to his endeavours only by behaving according to this God-sent Constitution.

Divine Guidance for humanity has been provided in two forms, the Word of God and the character of His Messengers, both forms being complementary to each other. The Message remains uninterpreted, mystical and non-practical without the Messenger, and the Messenger, without the Message, may be deified by those to whom he is sent.

The Prophet Muḥammad (peace be upon him) proclaimed the following in his sermon on the occasion of his Last *Ḥajj*: 'I am leaving you with two things which if you adhere to, you will never go astray. One is the Book of Allah – the Qur'ān. The other is my *Sunnah.'*

Hence the Muslim *Ummah* is bound to follow both the Book and the *Sunnah*. To leave one is to revolt against Divine Guidance. All the injunctions of God are appealing and beneficial to man. These injunctions lay down the foundation of an ideal society with morality as an off-shoot of these orders. The fear of eternal chastisement and the wish for eternal bliss motivate Muslims to surrender to the Will of God. Virtues and morality are based upon this concept. This is the focal point which provides the rationale for rejecting such forces as lust, greed and jealousy.

Of course, there are those who do not understand these principles, and many are the indignities and injustices which are heaped upon Islam due to this. It is important for the reader to remember that the word 'Muslim' denotes one who submits to the Will of God, while the collective term for such Muslims is *'Ummah'*. Therefore it must be understood that an individual or group of individuals purporting to be Muslim need not necessarily be so. It is by the actions of the individual or the group that the Qur'ān evaluates whether or not true submission to the Will of God is the motivation.

On the one hand, the wish for eternal bliss provides a wider base for moral behaviour, on the other, the fear of eternal chastisement consolidates that wider base of morality. Some of the components of social organisation in Islam are morality, simplicity, spontaneity, purity and austerity.

Islam adopts a reformative stance. All potentials are God-given. They can be fruitful only when they are utilised in accordance with the Will of God. Sovereignty belongs to Allah. Man is not sovereign, and it is destructive to regard him as such. In Islam everybody has the right to be a leader of his society. The man who obtains the support of the majority is entrusted with the administration of the society. All representatives have equal rights. This is the basis of democracy.

Islam provides a sound basis for the accumulation and distribution of wealth. All resources belong to Allah, over which every person has an equal right. There should be an ethical relationship between the consumer and the producer. This relationship should be governed by humility and benevolence. The mad rush for livelihood and accumulation of wealth makes man stone-hearted, thus he commits all sorts of offences for personal gain. These realities and revealed principles led me to follow Islam.

Islam provides a sound footing for economic reconstruction. There is a close relationship between spiritual and social life in Islam. Purification of the soul takes place in the social milieu and not in seclusion. Purity of thought is the bedrock of moral behaviour.

The pattern of domestic life propounded by Islam cannot be attained without purity of thought. The last Messenger of God, Muḥammad (peace be upon him), translated the Qur'ānic Revelations into practical reality by organising an unparalleled exemplary society.

Today, however, in spite of the acceptance of the Qur'ān as Revelation from Allah, the majority of Muslims have turned their faces against the directives of this great Book, hence the whole Muslim *Ummah* is downtrodden. The Prophet (peace be upon him) considered the Qur'ān as the emblem of the rise and fall of the Muslim *Ummah*: 'Allah will bestow success and dignity upon the people who act upon its teachings, and will cast those aside who neglect its teachings.' (Muslim)

Hence, for Muslims, there can be no way of life without the Qur'ān, which firmly influences the practices and efficacy of the *Ummah*. Today we have to adopt the same practices carried out by the first Muslims. The Prophet (peace be upon him) said: 'The best of you is the one who learns the Qur'ān and then teaches it to others.' (Bukhārī)

This modest effort aims to introduce the Qur'ān so that the reader may get a glimpse of the infinite excellence of this Book. Efforts have been made here to expound the teachings of the Qur'ān through its own words.

Sydney, Australia
August 1998 CE
Rabī' al-Thānī 1419H

Qazi Ashfaq Ahmad

Introduction

Once you know the Truth, the Absolute Reality, the Source of Life, the Path and the Destination, obviously you have a keen desire to convey it to others. Everyone naturally desires to share his/her happiness.

So, like others before me, after exploring Islam and experiencing glimpses of radiance from the Qur'ān, I have had the frequent desire for Muslims and non-Muslims to form an attachment to, and be touched by, the words of the Qur'ān. The Muslims who believe the Qur'ān to be the Word of God and have deep reverence for it as the Holy Book, interact with the Qur'ān in an entirely different manner from that of a non-Muslim who may not have any positive psychological conditioning as such.

In my experience, I find that very few non-Muslim friends get much help from the translations of the Qur'ān, given to them, for a better understanding of Islam. The Word of God, especially once it has been translated from its original Arabic, attracts only those exceptional people who are not given over solely to material pursuits and whose minds and hearts are still willing to pay attention to the spiritual order of life. Most others, however, do not take the Qur'ān seriously.

The Qur'ān, the Word of God, directly affects those who have a special bent of mind and mode of life – not, then, the general masses completely engrossed in materialism. There is a need to introduce the Qur'ān in a language and style comprehensible to the common man of the present era. The full text of the Qur'ān becomes more meaningful and understandable if one has the prerequisite of a non-materialistic outlook on life.

It is an arduous task to introduce the Qur'ān to mankind in this present era. Realising all my handicaps and limitations, I have taken the bold step of making an attempt to write such a book. This, my first attempt, is in the hope that scholars and people of great competence will be prompted to improve and make a comprehensible presentation of the Qur'ān for non-believers, in order that they may become aware of the Absolute Truth.

Originally, I had intended to prepare a small book for this purpose. However, after preparing the topics and discussing them with colleagues and scholars, it was considered more suitable to put together a more elaborate presentation defining the Qur'ān.

After my initial orientation towards Islam in 1950 when I was 20 years old, I have been engaged in two modes of Islamic living, one intellectual the other practical. I have been inspired on the one hand by Ḥamīduddīn Farāhī and Amīn Aḥsan Iṣlāḥī school of thought for an in-depth understanding of the Qur'ān, and by Sayyid Abu'l A'lā Mawdūdī on the other for the practical implementation of the Qur'ān, both for myself and *vis-à-vis* contemporary society. Two masterpieces, *Tadabbur-i-Qur'ān* by Amīn Aḥsan Iṣlāḥī and *Tafhīm al-Qur'ān* by Sayyid Mawdūdī have been my constant reference materials. In addition, I have consulted the following: *Fī Ẓilāl al-Qur'ān* by Sayyid Quṭb (1390 H); *Tafsīr al-Manār* by Muḥammad Rashīd Riḍā (1372 H); *Nayl al-Awṭār* by Muḥammad ibn 'Alī Ash-Shawkānī (1344 H); *Tāj al-'Arūs* by Murtaḍā az-Zabīdī (1205 H); *Al-Itqān fī 'Ulūm al-Qur'ān* by 'Abd ar-Raḥmān Jalāl-ad-Dīn as-Suyūṭī (911 H); *Tafsīr al-Qur'ān* by Abu'l Fidā' Ismā'īl ibn Kathīr (774 H); *Lisān al-'Arab* by Abu'l Faḍl Muḥammad ibn Mukarram ibn al-Manẓūr (711 H); *Anwār at-Tanzīl wa-Asrār at-Ta'wīl* by 'Abdullāh ibn 'Umar al-Bayḍāwī (691 H); *At-Tafsīr al-Kabīr* by Abu'l Faḍl Muḥammad Fakhruddīn ar-Rāzī (606 H); *Al-Kashshāf 'an Haqā'iq* by Maḥmūd ibn 'Umar az-Zamakhsharī (538 H); *Al-Mufradāt fī Gharīb al-Qur'ān* by Abu'l Qāsim

Ḥusayn ar-Rāghib (503 H); and *Jāmi' al-Bayān 'an Ta'wīl al-Qur'ān* by Abū Ja'far Muḥammad ibn Jarīr aṭ-Ṭabarī (310 H).

There are two different modes of the Word of Allah revealed to the last Prophet Muḥammad (peace be upon him). One is the order of Revelation of the verses over the course of 23 years, piecemeal, and the other is the order of compilation in the form of a book, the Qur'ān, known as the *Muṣḥaf.* Both modes are Divine and by their very nature highly important. This aspect of two different orders within the Qur'ān has not been thoroughly investigated and explained either to Believers or non-believers. It is a very important aspect, however, that must be dealt with extensively in any presentation – this at least for a full comprehension.

With this in mind the current work was written. It seeks to bring out the salient characteristics of the Qur'ān in general. The Holy Qur'ān is a Sacred Light for mankind with grandeur and purity of purpose. Without having training and the proper background for study of the Qur'ān, how is it possible for mere humanity to come close to understanding and utilising such a Message wherein can be achieved a practical human goal? One must be inspired when encountered by the record of the Message and the Messenger, Holy Witness to the Greatness, the Mercy and the Graciousness of Almighty Allah in His great plan to rescue mankind from darkness and ignorance. From the oft-repeated words, *Bismillāhir Raḥmānir Raḥīm,* to its doctrinal themes and its revelation, the Holy Qur'ān has been given to mankind for knowledge and instruction in every conceivable field of human endeavour. The last chapter of the present work gives suggestions to beginners about how to undertake a serious study of the Qur'ān. It is mostly useful for those who make efforts to attain Faith.

It is expected that if a non-believer goes through this book patiently with a serious frame of mind, he/she will appreciate the greatness and importance of the Qur'ān even to the extent of receiving Guidance from Allah to open his/her heart to

Islam. We pray that persons of noble character and conduct come forward and become motivated to accept Islam and serve it in a much better and effective way than those who are born Muslims.

It is the intention of the Author to present the knowledge of this great Message from the Lord of the Worlds in such a way that one may realise that it has been given to mankind to instruct according to the capability of the one who makes the quest. No sincere seeker after the Truth will go unrewarded when turning to the Holy Qur'ān, the best of books.

CHAPTER ONE

Bismillāhir Raḥmānir Raḥīm

(In the name of Allah, Most Gracious, Most Merciful)

He or she who opens the Qur'ān for the first time will be impressed by the fact that at the beginning of all but one of the *sūrahs* (chapters) is the Arabic phrase, *Bismillāhir Raḥmānir Raḥīm*. The English translation of these words is: In the name of God, Most Gracious, Most Merciful.

What is the significance of this Arabic phrase which is accorded so much importance in the Qur'ān and the *Sunnah*? In order to establish the influence and import of the Qur'ān, the preserved Word of Allah, and the necessity for the individual to read and receive Guidance, it is also necessary to study this phrase, the essence of which pervades the entirety of the Holy Book.

The Divine Attributes of Perfection

Allah comprises within Himself all the attributes of Perfection and represents, therefore, the Ultimate Reality:

And of Allah are all the Attributes of Perfection.

(Al-A'rāf, 7: 180)

The Arabic word *Ism* is primarily a word which is applied to describe the substance or the attribute of a being under consideration.

> *He imparted the knowledge of all the names to Adam.*
> (Al-Baqarah, 2: 31)

It denotes man's faculty for logical definition and, thus, of conceptual thinking. By 'Adam', the whole of humanity is meant here.

An Invocation

Bismillāhir Raḥmānir Raḥīm is a benediction with which every Muslim should commence any task, in order to receive the blessings of Allah. When these words are uttered with intention and full understanding, the following benefits are obtained:

1. The person becomes aware that the work to be done should not be against the orders of Allah.
2. The person receives encouragement and is given inspiration from Allah's two great virtues – Graciousness and Mercy. He/she receives the blessings of Allah and is, thus, saved from temptation.

Commencing with *Bismillāh* – Its History

The Qur'ān reveals that Allah taught mankind to use this invocation from the very beginning on more than one occasion, at times using slight variations of the formula, as in the following:

> *So he said (unto his followers): Embark in this (ship)! In the name of Allah be its run and its riding at anchor! Behold, my Sustainer is indeed Much-Forgiving, a Dispenser of Grace.*
> (Hūd, 11: 41)

Behold, it is from Solomon, and it says, 'In the name of Allah, the Most Gracious, the Dispenser of Grace.'

(An-Naml, 27: 30)

Read in the name of your Sustainer, Who has created. Created man out of a germ cell.

(Al-'Alaq, 96: 1–2)

Every *sūrah* except *at-Tawbah* (also known as *al-Barā'ah*) commences with this formula. Let it be noted that *at-Tawbah* heralded the withdrawal of benevolence extended to the pagan Quraysh who were opposed to Islam.

There are two schools of thought regarding *Bismillāhir Raḥmānir Raḥīm*. The scholars of Makkah and Kufah believe it to be a verse of the *sūrahs*, while the scholars of Madinah, Basrah and Syria say that it should be recited before commencing to read the Qur'ān.

Every important affair commenced without the name of Allah shall remain incomplete.

(Muslim and Bukhārī)

The Three Names of Allah: Allāh, *Raḥmān* and *Raḥīm*

Allāh

Allah, the Supreme Being, is the Creator of the heavens and the earth. Even the pagan Arabs acknowledged Him as the Greatest. They considered gods and goddesses as the agents of Allah. From the very beginning this name has been assigned to God, the Lord and Creator.

Say: 'Who provides for you from heaven and earth?
Who has endowed you with sight and hearing?
Who brings forth the living from the dead, and
the dead from the living? Who ordains all things?'
And they will surely answer: 'It is Allah.'

Say: 'Will you not then become conscious of Him? Such is Allah, your Sustainer, the Ultimate Truth. For, after the Truth (has been forsaken), what is there left but error? How can you turn away from Him?'

(Yūnus, 10: 31–2)

If you ask them who it is who has created the heavens and the earth and subjected the sun and the moon, they will say, 'Allah.' How then can they turn away from Him? Allah gives abundantly to whom He wills, and sparingly to whom He pleases. He has knowledge of all things. If you ask them who it is that sends down water from the sky and thereby quickens the earth after its death, they will reply: 'Allah.'

Say: 'Praise, then, be to Allah!' But most of them do not understand.

(Al-'Ankabūt, 29: 61–3)

Yet if you ask them who created them, they will promptly reply that it was Allah. How can they turn away from Him?

(Az-Zukhruf, 43: 87)

Believers, remember Allah frequently: praise Him morning and evening. He and His angels bless you, so that He may lead you from darkness to the light. He is merciful to true believers.

(Al-Aḥzāb, 33: 41–3)

Amīr al-Mu'minīn 'Alī (*ra*) narrated in *Kitāb al-Tawḥīd* of *Tafsīr al-Imām* that Allah is the Being to Whom human beings call for help when all their hopes are shattered.

Raḥmān and Raḥīm

We must look closely at these two attributes of Allah, *ar-Raḥmān* and *ar-Raḥīm*. Both are derived from the same root, '*Raḥmah*' meaning mercy and kindness. Both are attributes of Allah.'*Raḥmān*' indicates the spontaneous and intensive benevolence of Allah. Creation is the manifestation of His Mercy.

Raḥīm, on the other hand, depicts the permanence of the Mercy bestowed upon the universe. This permanence is observed in the supervision, control and sustenance provided by Allah, defined as His Mercy.

The Qur'ān, the Guidance from Allah, the *Raḥmān* and the *Raḥīm,* is a result of His Benevolence, and the understanding and practice of the Qur'ān, is to be attained because of His Mercy by the person who believes in Him with all His attributes.

> *The Most Gracious has imparted this Qur'ān (unto man). He has created man. He has imparted unto him articulate thought and speech.*
>
> (Ar-Raḥmān, 55: 1–4)

The epithet *Ar-Raḥmān* (the Most Gracious) has intense significance. It denotes the unconditional, all-embracing quality and exercise of Grace and Mercy and is applied exclusively to Allah, 'Who has willed upon Himself the Law of Grace and Mercy.'

> *Say: 'To whom belongs all that the heavens and the earth contain? Say: 'To Allah. He has decreed mercy for Himself, and will gather you all on the Day of Resurrection: that day is sure to come . . .'*
>
> (Al-An'ām, 6: 12)

> *When those that believe in Our Revelations come to you, say: 'Peace be upon you. Your Lord has decreed Mercy on Himself. If any one of you commits evil through ignorance and then repents and mends his ways, then He is Forgiving, Merciful.'*
>
> (Al-An'ām, 6: 54)

Kataba 'alā nafsihī ar-Raḥmah (He decreed mercy on Himself) is mentioned twice as above in the Qur'ān, referring to His Grace and Mercy (*Raḥmah*). None of the other attributes are described in such a way.

Raḥmān as seen in this world, for the here and now, sustains all human beings even those who become disloyal to Him. *Raḥīm,* as preparation for the Next World, gives to Believers much reward. Non-believers, He calls gently towards Islam in order to save them from the fire of Hell.

Summing Up

Bismillāhir Raḥmānir Raḥīm is the most powerful tool of hope for all Muslims and should be recognised as such. As long as Muslims realise that they have Allah to turn to in times of sorrow and to remember in times of joy and happiness, that if they practise the requirements of Islam to the best of their ability, they have grasped the true spirit of this magnificent phrase.

Directives

1. Guidance, total guidance, comes with the pronouncement of the name of Allah, Most Gracious, Most Merciful.
2. He is Allah to Whom His servants return. He is the Most Gracious, Who has opened the way of His All-Encompassing Mercy for Believers and disbelievers alike, the mercy which provides them with all that is necessary and good for their existence in this life.
3. He is Most Merciful, Who has reserved His Special Mercy for Believers; that mercy which ensures their happiness in the life Hereafter, and their nearness to their Lord.

Conclusion

1. This present *Jāhiliyyah* (Time of Ignorance) differs from the previous one, in the sense that man now considers himself as God. In the previous *Jāhiliyyah*, God/Allah, was acknowledged, but partners were ascribed to Him.

Presently man believes in *Lā Ilāha* (no God) but not in *Illallāh* (except Allah). In the past, belief was in Allah but not in *Lā Ilāha*.

2. We should begin all our actions with the name of Allah and express our Prayers, gratitude and servitude in the manner required by Allah.
3. We have to fully comprehend all the attributes of Allah, especially the ones mentioned in *Sūrah* Al-Fātiḥah, the opening *sūrah* of the Qur'ān.

CHAPTER TWO

Revelation – The Word of God

2.1 The Absolute Truth

The Baghwad Gīta, the Torah, the Bible, the Qur'ān – all of these books are religious sources, or codes to which their followers have referred for centuries. All of them being inspirations in one way or another to different people, different communities, all of them giving lessons in human conduct and morality through stories and parables.

The words of the Qur'ān are recited at least five times a day, every day, by more than one-fifth of mankind. The Qur'ān is quoted orally, or in writing, studied or committed to memory, in whole or in part, much more than any other religious or non-religious book.

The Qur'ān is the last Revealed Word of God (Allah), revealed in the Arabic language to Prophet Muḥammad (peace be upon him) in the period 610 to 632 CE. It is the basic source of Islamic teachings and law. It contains guidance, principles and doctrines for every sphere of human activity. The Qur'ān acts as a practical handbook on various issues relating to social life, marriage, inheritance, penal law, and international law. Throughout its pages, it appeals to the reason of man and urges every person to follow its teachings, convincing each individual of his/her personal responsibility and accountability.

The Qur'ān is an eternal Message and at its fountainhead, God is eternal, for ever and ever. It is a Message for all times, for all climes and countries. It is a Message not only for Muslims but for all mankind. The Qur'ān is not the first Message of God but is actually the final version. Its mission was not to introduce a new Message but to endorse, with fresh vigour, the Message delivered earlier to other Prophets such as Abraham, Moses, David and Jesus who respectively received the Scrolls, the Torah, the Psalms, and the Gospels.

The Qur'ān, being the last revealed book, takes stock of previous religions and makes reference to some important peoples and countries of the world. These references are testified to by quotations from the Bible and classical authors, and corroborated by archaeological researches. It is gratifying to note that several European Orientalists have taken the trouble to explore Arabia, tracing the relics of her glorious past, discovering her monuments and deciphering their inscriptions. Their explorations and researches have confirmed the Qur'ānic description of peoples and countries.

The Qur'ān is devoid of any human interference, interpolation and interjection. Nobody, be it the Prophet (peace be upon him) himself, rulers, governments, scholars or otherwise has had the audacity to change one word, in the form of addition or deletion, from the Holy Book. Chief Justice of Andhra Pradesh High Court and the former Vice Chancellor of Osmania University in India, gave the following comment at the release function of its Telgu Translation in Hyderabad, India on 31 December 1995: 'During the Caliphate of 'Uthmān (*ra*) due to regional and geographical factors, the believers recited the Qur'ān with different accents. 'Uthmān (*ra*) had one standard copy prepared and distributed throughout the countries, after withdrawing the former copies. The Qur'ān, thereafter, was restricted to the copy thus prepared and from that time onwards the standard version has been used without change in words or order or even punctuations.'

2.2 The Qur'ān Defines Itself

The Qur'ān is the Word of God

> *Ḥa Mīm. The bestowal from on High (of this revelation) issues from the Most Gracious, the Dispenser of Grace: a divine writ, the messages whereof have been clearly spelled out as a discourse in the Arabic tongue for people of (innate) knowledge, to be a herald of glad tidings as well as a warning. And yet (whenever this divine writ is offered to men), most of them turn away so that they cannot hear (its message).*
>
> (Fuṣṣilat, 41: 1–4)

Every one of Allah's Prophets was entrusted with a Message in his own people's tongue, *'so that he might make (the Truth) clear unto them'* (Ibrāhīm, 14: 4). The Qur'ān was revealed as an '*Arabic ordinance*' (Ar-Ra'd, 13: 37) so as to enable the Arabian Prophet Muḥammad (peace be upon him) to propound it to the people of his immediate environment and through them, to the whole world. The Message of the Qur'ān is meant to impress upon everyone who listens to or reads it directly in Arabic or through its translation/commentary as an appeal, directed, primarily, to man's reason, and that 'feeling' alone can never provide a sufficient basis of faith. That the Message of the Qur'ān is universal, and not restricted to the Arabs alone, is brought out clearly in the following verse:

> *Say (O Prophet): O mankind; Verily I am sent forth to you all by Allah.*
>
> (Al-A'rāf, 7: 158)

These are the people of knowledge who understand the innermost meaning of Divine Revelation and therefore submit to its guidance. People who are devoid of such knowledge, pay no attention and hence, the Qur'ān is meaningless to them.

The Book of Guidance and Criterion

> *It was the month of Ramaḍān in which the Qur'ān was (first) revealed as a guidance unto man, as a self-evident proof of that guidance and as the criterion by which to discern the true from the false.*
>
> (Al-Baqarah, 2: 185)

Three main characteristics of the Qur'ān are mentioned in this verse. The Creator and Sustainer of the Universe, Allah, in addition to providing material amenities to His most important creation – mankind – also provides them with guidance about the most appropriate lifestyle for them. In order to satisfy the rational faculty of human beings Allah supplemented this guidance with evidence. Moreover, Allah explicitly narrated instances of right and wrong in order to develop a criterion, and to provide insight such that the correct and incorrect ways for leading one's life in this world could be differentiated.

The Book Without any Contradiction

> *Will they not ponder over the Qur'ān? If it had been from any other than Allah, they could have surely found in it many contradictions.*
>
> (An-Nisā', 4: 82)

This characteristic of being 'free from all inner contradiction' nullifies the idea of the Qur'ān as authored by the Prophet Muḥammad (peace be upon him) himself. Opponents of Islam had levelled the charge that Muḥammad (peace be upon him) had composed the Qur'ān in stages during his lifetime and as suited his changing personal and political requirements.

The Qur'ān challenges these opponents, stating that there is no contradiction in the concepts and statements made in the Qur'ān. If a human being had coined words and made statements over a period of 23 years, it would have been impossible for him not to contradict himself. Hence, the coordination and unity of thought evident in the Qur'ān is one of the proofs that the Qur'ān is the compilation of the revealed Words of God.

The Book of Reference for Legal Matters

> *O you who have attained faith! Do not ask about matters which, if they were to be made manifest to you (in terms of law) might cause you hardship; for, if you should ask about them while the Qur'ān is being revealed, they might (indeed) be made manifest to you (as laws).*
>
> (Al-Mā'idah, 5: 101)

The Qur'ān is not a detailed Book of law or codes. Its basic task is to develop insight, leading to the Right Way and enabling people to frame the details for living in this world. Allah directs the Believers, the followers of the Prophet Muḥammad (peace be upon him) as He directed the followers of Prophet Moses, that they should not go on demanding proof from Allah. They should use their discretion in order to adjust themselves to the dynamic, changing world. The Qur'ān should be taken as the Book of reference for legal matters, and not as a book of detailed rules and regulations regarding society.

This verse directs Believers not to create 'additional' laws from the injunctions clearly laid down as such by the Qur'ān, since this 'might cause hardship'. The followers of the Prophet Moses suffered because they put too many questions to their Prophet and thereupon disagreed about the Prophet's teachings. In the last portion of this verse Allah informs us that by leaving certain matters unspoken, He has left them to a person's discretion, thus providing the opportunity to act in accordance with one's conscience and in the best interests of the community.

Guidance is not for Non-Believers

> *Even if there be a Qur'ān by which the mountains could be removed or the earth cleft asunder or the dead made to speak, (they will not believe). But to Allah is the power over everything. Do those who believe not know that had Allah willed He could have guided all people?*
>
> (Ar-Ra'd, 13: 31)

The two propositions, Allah's knowledge of the future and man's free-will, seem to contradict one another. But we human beings are working under constraints of time while Allah is independent of time. Hence, His knowledge of the future should not be taken as predestination, opposing man's free-will. The very concept of morality and moral responsibility presupposes free-will on man's part. Had Allah so willed, every human being would have been forced to live righteously thus depriving man of this free-will and morality of its meaning.

Thus, Allah grants man the freedom to choose between right and wrong. He guides all who turn to Him and are true to their bond with Him but He also withholds His guidance from those who break their bond with Him.

A Book of Clear Discourse and the Best of Narratives

> *Alif, Lām, Rā. These are the Messages of a revelation of a discourse clear in itself and clearly showing the truth. We have revealed it (as a discourse) in the Arabic language, so that you might encompass it with your reason. In the measure that We reveal this Qur'ān unto you (O Prophet) We explain it to you through the best of narratives, and before this you were indeed among those who were unaware (of what revelation is).*
>
> (Yūsuf, 12: 1–3)

Two different but complementary attributes of the Qur'ān are mentioned in this verse. The first is that the Qur'ān is self-explanatory. The verses are clear and obvious, with further enlightenment being afforded as one part offers explanation of the other. Second, the Qur'ān has been set forth in the best way not only in content but in its manner as well. The Qur'ānic verses were expanded gradually as Revelation went on.

A Book of Glad Tidings to Believers

> *Ṭā Sīn. These are the Messages of the Qur'ān – a divine writ clear in itself and clearly showing the truth: a guidance and a glad tiding to the believers who are constant in Prayer and spend in charity: for it is, they who in their hearts are certain of the life to come!*
>
> (An-Naml, 27: 1–3)

The Qur'ān, by clearly promising the Believers entry into Paradise in the eternal life of the Hereafter, is a source of glad tidings. One who believes in its verses, should carry on his/her mission, however difficult or full of suffering it may be, with the full satisfaction and contentment of receiving reward in the Next Life.

A Book of Wisdom

> *Yā Sīn. Consider this Qur'ān full of wisdom: verily, you are indeed one of Allah's message-bearers pursuing a straight path. This is a revelation of the Mighty One, the Merciful, so that you may warn people whose forefathers had not been warned, and who therefore are unaware (of the meaning of right and wrong).*
>
> (Yā Sīn, 36: 1–6)

The literal translation is 'the wise Qur'ān'. It obviously means that the words of the Qur'ān, if understood properly, impart wisdom and clarify the vision of its readers. The statement of declaring Muḥammad (peace be upon him) as Allah's Messenger, after expressing the wisdom to be found in the Qur'ān, clearly indicates that the logical consequence of obtaining wisdom from the Qur'ān leads a person to believe in the prophethood of Muḥammad (peace be upon him).

Hearts are Locked if they do not Ponder Over the Qur'ān

> *Will they not then, ponder over this Qur'ān? Or are there locks upon their hearts?*
>
> (Muḥammad 47: 24)

All laws of nature are instituted by Allah, hence they may be termed *sunnat Allāh* (the way of Allah). One law is that a person who persistently adheres to false beliefs and refuses to listen to the voice of Truth gradually loses the ability to perceive the Truth. Thus, a seal is finally set upon his heart.

The Qur'ān – Step-by-Step Revelation

> *Nay, I call to witness the setting of the stars – and behold, this is indeed a most solemn affirmation, if you but knew it! Behold, it is a truly glorious Qur'ān, (conveyed unto man) in a well-guarded divine writ which none may touch except the purified: a revelation from the Sustainer of all the worlds! Would you now, look down with disdain on a tiding like this, and make it your provision to call the Truth a lie?*
>
> (Al-Wāqi'ah, 56: 75–82)

The Qur'ān was revealed to the Prophet (peace be upon him) as he carried out his mission of 'full submission to Allah – the One and only One Lord' to inspire, encourage and direct the task assigned to him.

The Qur'ān Demands Thoughtful Consideration

> *O you enwrapped one! Keep awake (in Prayer) at night, all but a small part of one-half thereof – or make it a*

> *little less than that or add to it (at will); and (during that time) recite the Qur'ān calmly and distinctly, with your mind attuned to its meaning.*
>
> (Al-Muzzammil, 73: 1–4)

The Prophet (peace be upon him), being very enthusiastic, used to recite the Qur'ān hurriedly lest he might forget. Allah assured him that the words of the Qur'ān were to be preserved and so he should not be anxious about its memorisation. So he was ordered by Allah to recite it calmly with measured utterance giving thoughtful consideration to its meaning for correct implementation. Though the address here is to the Prophet (peace be upon him), it should nevertheless be taken as a directive to all those who want to act upon Allah's instructions.

2.3 The Qur'ān Assigns Itself Other Names

As advised by my teacher, I myself experienced that many of the expressions, phrases or ideas not initially clear became clear while going through the Qur'ān. Principles, notions and directions are elaborated in the Qur'ān itself at different places. The function and role of the Qur'ān becomes comprehensible if we go through the other names of the Qur'ān as given in the Qur'ān itself.

Al-Kitāb – The Divine Writ

The Qur'ān is the divine writ, the one revealed after the Bible. In the course of its history, the Bible has been subjected to considerable and frequent arbitrary alterations. It is also a fact that many of the laws enunciated in the Qur'ān differ from those of the Bible. Confirmation of the Bible by the Qur'ān refers only to the basic Truths still contained in the Bible, and not to its time-bound legislation or to its present text. It should be kept in mind that the word 'scripture' or 'gospel' as mentioned in the Qur'ān is not identical with the four Gospels of today but instead refers to an original, since lost, Revelation bestowed upon Jesus and known to his contemporaries under its Greek name of Evangelion (good tidings), on which the Arabic word *Injīl* is based.

> *This divine writ is not to be doubted. It is a guide for the righteous.*
>
> (Al-Baqarah, 2: 2)

> *Would you enjoin righteousness to others and forget it yourselves? Yet you read the Scriptures. Have you no sense?*
>
> (Al-Baqarah, 2: 44)

> *There are illiterate men among them who, ignorant of the Scriptures, know of nothing except lies and vague fancies.*
>
> (Al-Baqarah, 2: 78)

> *He has revealed to you the divine writ with the truth, confirming what preceded it; and He has already revealed the Torah and the Gospel.*
>
> (Āl 'Imrān, 3: 3)

> *It is He Who has revealed to you the divine writ. Some of its verses are precise in meaning, they are the foundation of the Book, and others allegorical. Those whose hearts are infected with disbelief follow the allegorical part, so as to create dissension and to misinterpret it. But no one knows its interpretation except Allah. And those who are well-grounded in knowledge say: 'We believe in it, the whole of it is from our Lord:' and none will grasp the Message except men of understanding.*
>
> (Āl 'Imrān, 3: 7)

Al-Kitāb al-Ḥakīm – The Book of Wisdom

The Arabic word *al-Ḥakīm* means the wise one for an animated being. The Qur'ān uses this word with reference to its content. This has the connotation of imparting wisdom.

Each verse of the Qur'ān as well as the Qur'ān as a whole is full of wisdom. For the Qur'ān, the word *al-Ḥakīm* means having deep and practical knowledge of nature and human nature.

> *Alif, Lām, Rā. These are the verses of the Book of Wisdom.*
> (Yūnus, 10: 1)

> *These are the revelations of the Wise Book.*
> (Luqmān, 31: 2)

Hudā – Guidance

The Qur'ān is the touchstone in deciding what is genuine and what is false in the earlier Scriptures.

The Creator of human beings knows human nature best. Human beings cannot know human nature in its totality but they can find it out partially by scientific pursuit. According to Islam, mankind was in need of guidance from the Creator. Hence, Allah bestowed this upon humanity from the very beginning. Divine Guidance is divided into three categories. First, it is in the form of *dīn*, the basic, unchanging Truths which have been preached by every one of God's Messengers. Second, it is in the form of *Sharī'ah*, a system of law necessary for a community's social and spiritual welfare. Third, it is the *minhāj*, an open road or a way of life, principles based on *dīn* and *Sharī'ah*.

The *dīn* in Islam is the same call preached by each Messenger of God while the *Sharī'ah* and *minhāj*, promulgated and recommended by the Prophets, varies in accordance with the exigencies of the time and of each community's cultural development.

> *This Book is not to be doubted. It is a guidance for the righteous.*
> (Al-Baqarah, 2: 2)

> *Say: 'Whoever is an enemy of Gabriel!' For surely he has brought it down by Allah's grace to your heart,*

confirming what was (revealed) earlier and a guidance and good tidings to the believers.

(Al-Baqarah, 2: 97)

The month of Ramaḍān is the month in which the Qur'ān was revealed, a Book of guidance (hudā) for mankind with proofs of guidance distinguishing right from wrong. Therefore, whoever of you is well in that month, let him fast. But he who is ill or on a journey shall fast a similar number of days later on.

(Al-Baqarah, 2: 185)

After those Prophets We sent forth 'Īsā (Jesus), the son of Maryam (Mary), confirming the Torah already revealed, and gave him the Gospel, in which there is guidance and light, corroborating that which was revealed before it in the Torah, a guide and an admonition to the righteous.

(Al-Mā'idah, 5: 46)

Then to Mūsā We gave the Book to complete Our blessing for him who does good (by following it) and (to make) plain all things, and (to provide) guidance and mercy, so that his people might believe in the ultimate meeting with their Lord.

(Al-An'ām, 6: 154)

O mankind! an admonition has come to you from your Lord, a healing for what is in the hearts, a guide and a blessing to true believers.

(Yūnus, 10: 57)

A guidance and a blessing to the righteous.

(Luqmān, 31: 3)

Mubīn – Makes Things Very Clear

Just like the word *Ḥakīm*, the word *Mubīn* is used both in qualifying the name as well as describing its function. Hence '*mubīn*' means 'clear, manifest, obvious' as the qualification of the noun. It also means making clear a manifest Truth. Both these meanings apply to the Qur'ān. The Qur'ān is clear in itself and clearly shows the Truth.

> *Alif. Lām. Rā. These are the verses of the Book which clearly indicates (right and wrong).*
>
> (Al-Ḥijr, 15: 1)

> *These are the verses of the Book which clearly indicates (right and wrong).*
>
> (Ash-Shu'arā', 26: 2)

> *Ṭā. Sīn. These are the verses of the Qur'ān, the Book which indicates (right and wrong).*
>
> (An-Naml, 27: 1)

Shifā' – Healing

The Qur'ān is a remedy for all that is contrary to Truth and moral good. The Qur'ān is not much use to the evil-doers, those who, out of selfishness or an excessive love of this world, reject outright any suggestion of Divine Guidance.

> *O mankind! an admonition has come to you from your Lord, a healing for what is in the hearts, a guide and a blessing to true believers.*
>
> (Yūnus, 10: 57)

> *We reveal of the Qur'ān that which is a healing and mercy to true believers, though it adds nothing but ruin to the evil-doers.*
>
> (Al-Isrā', 17: 82)

> *Had We revealed the Qur'ān in a foreign tongue they would have said: 'If only its verses were expounded! Why in a foreign tongue, (when) the Prophet is Arabian?' Say: 'To the true believers it is a guide and a healing balm. But those who believe not, there is deafness in their ears and blindness in their eyes. They are like men called from afar.'*
>
> (Fuṣṣilat, 41: 44)

Kitāb-un-Maknūn – A Book Well-Guarded

The well-guarded tablet is taken by some in a literal sense so considering it an actual 'heavenly tablet' (*'lawḥ maḥfūẓ*) upon which the Qur'ān is inscribed for eternity. Generally, it is taken as an allusion to the imperishable quality of this divine writ used metaphorically. The phrase 'upon a well-guarded tablet' relates to Allah's promise that the Qur'ān will never be corrupted, and that it will be free of all arbitrary additions and dimunitions '*in a Book well-guarded*'.

(Al-Wāqi'ah, 56: 78)

> *Nay, but this is the glorious Qur'ān upon an imperishable tablet (preserved).*

(Al-Burūj, 85: 21–2)

This prophecy is confirmed by the fact that the text of the Qur'ān has remained free from all alterations, additions or deletions ever since it was recited by the Prophet (peace be upon him) in the seventh century of the Christian era. There is no other instance of any book, of whatever description, which has been similarly preserved over such a length of time.

> *It is We ourselves Who have bestowed from on High this reminder and it is We who shall truly guard it (from all corruption).*

(Al-Ḥijr, 15: 9)

Al-Ḥaqq – Truth

The Qur'ān frequently points out that the basic ethical Truths enunciated in it are the same as those of earlier Revelations. The irreligious mind is always against the idea of Divine Revelation and of man's absolute dependence on and responsibility to God, the Ultimate Cause of all that exists.

> *And now that they have received from Us the Truth, they ask: 'Why is he not given the like of what was given to Mūsā?' But do they not deny what was given to Mūsā? They say: 'Two works of magic supporting*

one another!' And they declare: 'We will believe in neither of them.'

(Al-Qaṣaṣ, 28: 48)

We have revealed to you the Book in Truth (for the instruction) of mankind. He that follows the right path shall follow it to his own advantage; and he that goes astray shall do so at his own peril. You are not their custodian.

(Az-Zumar, 39: 41)

Bashīr – Giver of Glad Tidings

The Qur'ān, if taken seriously and acted upon, opens ways for happiness and contentment. It is full of directives which, when implemented, bring prosperity and happiness. This is the glad tidings of which the Prophet (peace be upon him) spoke about to the listeners of the Qur'ān.

Say: 'Whoever is an enemy of Gabriel!' For surely he has brought it down by Allah's grace to your heart, confirming what was (revealed) earlier and a guidance and good tidings to the believers.

(Al-Baqarah, 2: 97)

(He has made it) unswerving from the Truth, so that he may give warning of a dire scourge from Him, proclaim to the faithful who do good works that a rich and everlasting reward awaits them.

(Al-Kahf, 18: 2)

It is good news and a warning: yet most of them turn away and give no heed.

(Fuṣṣilat, 41: 4)

Tadhkirah – Reminder

The Qur'ān reminds its readers of the existence and omnipotence of Allah. Thus the Qur'ān is a reminder because it brings into the full light of consciousness the instinctive realisation of Allah's existence which in general is hazy and unconscious. According to the Qur'ān, the ability to perceive the existence of the Supreme Power is innate in human nature and it is this instinctive cognition that makes every sane human being bear witness about himself.

> *Nay, verily these (messages) are but a reminder and so, whosoever is willing may remember Him.*
>
> ('Abasa, 80: 11–12)

> *And whenever your Sustainer brings forth their offspring from the loins of the children of Adam, He (thus) calls upon them to bear witness about themselves: 'Am I not your Sustainer?' – to which they answer: 'Yes indeed, we do bear witness!'*
>
> (Al-A'rāf, 7: 172)

> *Therefore, let him who will, keep it in remembrance.*
>
> ('Abasa, 80: 12)

Mukarramah, Marfū'ah and Muṭahharah – Honoured, Exalted and Purified

The Qur'ān is purified from all kinds of false ideas and thoughts. It presents nothing but the pure Truth. The angels assigned to convey the words of Allah to the Prophet (peace be upon him) guarded the verses and conveyed them intact.

> *It is written in scrolls, which are honoured, exalted, purified, (and which) are written by the noble and virtuous scribes.*
>
> ('Abasa, 80: 13–16)

Al-Furqān – The Criterion

Al-Furqān is the criterion based on religious knowledge and understanding, which enables a person to distinguish between Truth and falsehood, right and wrong. Divine

Revelation, the expression of the Will of Allah, i.e. the Qur'ān is the true standard of right and wrong.

> *The month of Ramaḍān is the month in which the Qur'ān was revealed, a book of guidance for mankkind with proofs of guidance distinguishing right from wrong. Therefore, whoever of you is well in that month, let him fast. But he who is ill or on a journey shall fast a similar number of days later on.*
>
> (Al-Baqarah, 2: 185)

> *Before this, as a guide to mankind, He sent down the Criterion (of judgement between right and wrong). Then those who reject Faith in the Signs of Allah will suffer the severest penalty, and Allah is Exalted in Might, and He is the Lord of Retribution.*
>
> (Āl 'Imrān, 3: 4)

> *Blessed be He Who has revealed Al-Furqān (the Criterion) to His servant, that he may be a warner to all mankind.*
>
> (Al-Furqān, 25: 1)

Al-Bayyināt – Signs

Two prototypes of signs are mentioned in the Qur'ān as being given to Prophet Muḥammad (peace be upon him). The first is the Qur'ān itself, and the second the very life of the Prophet as an illustration of the Qur'ān.

> *And We granted them manifest Signs in affairs (of religion): it was only after knowledge had been granted to them that they disagreed among themselves out of evil motives. On the Day of Resurrection your Lord Himself will judge their differences.*
>
> (Al-Jāthiyah, 45: 17)

> *It is He Who brings down manifest revelations to His servant, so that He may lead you out of darkness into the light. Allah is Compassionate and Merciful to you.*
>
> (Al-Ḥadīd, 57: 9)

Tanzīl – Revelation

The words of the Qur'ān, 'no falsehood can approach it', rule out any misinterpretation. The verses of the Qur'ān cannot be openly changed by means of additions or omissions, nor surreptitiously, by hostile or deliberately confusing interpretations.

> *Verily, this is a Revelation from the Lord of the Worlds.*
> (Ash-Shu'arā', 26: 192)

> *It is a Revelation sent down by (Him), the Exalted in Might, Most Merciful.*
> (Yā Sīn, 36: 5)

> *A Revelation from (Allah), Most Gracious, Most Merciful.*
> (Fuṣṣilat, 41: 2)

> *No falsehood can approach it from before or behind it. It is a revelation from One Full of Wisdom, worthy of Praise.*
> (Fuṣṣilat, 41: 42)

Nūr – Light

Light itself is manifest and illuminates everything that is hidden in the darkness around it. So, the Qur'ān is also the light, being based as it is on the Truth. Therefore, by this light of the Qur'ān, mankind can understand and solve all kinds of problems.

> *Those who follow the Messenger, the unlettered Prophet, whom they shall find mentioned in the Torah and the Gospel. He will enjoin righteousness upon them and forbid them to do evil. He will make good things lawful to them and prohibit all that is bad (and impure). He will relieve them of their burdens and of the shackles that weigh upon them. Those that believe in him and honour him, those that help him, and follow the Light which is sent down with him – it is they who will prosper.*
> (Al-A'rāf, 7: 157)

Believe then in Allah and His Messenger and in the light which We have revealed. Allah has knowledge of all your actions.

(At-Taghābun, 64: 8)

Burhān – Convincing Proof

The Qur'ān, because of its rational approach and convincing argument is in itself a proof that it has been bestowed upon mankind by Allah.

O mankind! You have received clear proof from your Lord. We have sent forth to you a light (that is) manifest.

(An-Nisā', 4: 174)

Maw'izah – Direction of Advice

Allah's admonitions and directives are a curse for those who do wrong because they have a spiritual disease in their hearts. Allah directs their lives and provides a healing for their spiritual disease.

O mankind! There has come to you a direction from your Lord and a healing for the (diseases) in your hearts, a guide and a blessing to true believers.

(Yūnus, 10: 57)

Raḥmah – Mercy

All the facilities and bounties bestowed upon mankind by Allah result from His mercy. This Qur'ān, the guidance on how to live, is a result of His Benevolence and Mercy.

Then, to Mūsā We gave the Book, completing (Our favour) to those who would do right and explaining all things in detail – and a guide and a mercy, that they might believe in the ultimate meeting with their Lord.

(Al-An'ām, 6: 154)

> *O mankind! There has come to you a direction from your Lord and a healing for the (diseases) in your hearts, a guide and a blessing to true believers.*
>
> (Yūnus, 10: 57)

Āyāt – The Signs of Allah

The Qur'ānic term *āyah* sometimes denotes a miracle in the sense of a happening that goes beyond the usual course of nature. Generally though it denotes a 'sign' or 'message' in the Qur'ān. The Prophet's (peace be upon him) miracle is the Qur'ān itself – a message perfect in its lucidity and ethical worldview, destined for all times and all stages of human development, addressed not merely to the feelings but also to the minds of men, open to everyone, regardless of his race or social environment, and bound to remain unchanged forever.

> *This is a sūrah which We have revealed and sanctioned, proclaiming in it clear revelations, so that you may take heed.*
>
> (An-Nūr, 24: 1)

> *Let no one turn you away from Allah's revelations, now that they have been revealed to you. And invite (people) to your Lord, and be not of the company of those who join gods with Allah.*
>
> (Al-Qaṣaṣ, 28: 87)

> *So naught was the reply of Ibrāhīm's people except that they said: 'Kill him or burn him.' But from the fire Allah delivered him. Surely in this there are signs for true believers.*
>
> (Al-'Ankabūt, 29: 24)

> *They ask: 'Why has no Sign been given him by his Lord?' Say: 'Signs are in the hands of Allah. My mission is only to give plain warning.'*
>
> (Al-'Ankabūt, 29: 50)

Bear in mind the Signs of Allah which are recited in your houses and His wisdom. For Allah understands their finest mysteries and is well-acquainted (with them).

(Al-Aḥzāb, 33: 34)

To Him belong the keys of the heavens and the earth. Those who reject the Signs of Allah shall assuredly be in loss.

(Az-Zumar, 39: 63)

Nadhīr – Warner

For people who are devoid of knowledge and to whom, in consequence, the Qur'ān is meaningless, there are warnings from Allah in this respect. He uses the Prophet (peace be upon him) as the warner.

Give good news and admonition, yet most of them turn away, and so they hear not.

(Fuṣṣilat, 41: 4)

CHAPTER THREE

Doctrines

3.1 Paradigm Shift from the Mundane to the Magnificent

The Qur'ān, more than any other single phenomenon known to mankind, has fundamentally affected the religious, social and political history of the world. The Qur'ān extended its worldview far beyond the confines of Arabia and produced the first ideological society known to man; this through its insistence on consciousness and knowledge. It engendered among its followers a spirit of intellectual curiosity and independent enquiry, ultimately resulting in that splendid era of learning and scientific research which distinguished the world of Islam at the height of its cultural vigour.

The culture fostered by the Qur'ān penetrated in countless ways and sub-ways the mind of medieval Europe and gave rise to that revival of Western culture which we call the Renaissance. It became in the course of time largely responsible for the birth of what is described as the 'Age of Science', the age in which we live today. The very uniqueness of the Qur'ān consists in the fact that the more our worldly knowledge and historical experience increases, the more meanings, hitherto unsuspected, reveal themselves in its pages. No other sacred Scripture has ever had a similarly immediate impact upon the lives of the people who are new to its Message, and through them to the generations that followed, in the entire course of civilisation.

To the Believers, the Qur'ān represents the ultimate manifestation of Allah's grace to mankind, the ultimate wisdom, and the ultimate beauty of expression; in short, the true Word of Allah. The Qur'ān supplied to the Believers a basis for their ethical valuation and a direction for their worldly endeavours. It is still only the Qur'ān that provides a comprehensive answer to the question: 'How should I behave in order to achieve a good life in this world and happiness in the Life to Come?'

The Qur'ān, unlike all other sacred Scriptures, lays *stress on reason* as a valid way to faith and insists on the inseparability of the spiritual, physical and social spheres of human existence. Thus the Qur'ān is a guidance not only towards the spiritual good of the Hereafter but also towards a good spiritual, physical and social life attainable in this world.

The thesis of the Qur'ān is that all life, being given by Allah, is a unity and that the problems of the flesh and the mind, of sex and economies, of individual righteousness and social equity, are intimately connected with the hopes which man may legitimately entertain with regard to Life-after-Death.

Ethical Teachings of the Qur'ān

The descriptions of the Qur'ān and its references to historical circumstances and events, both at the time of the Prophet (peace be upon him) and in earlier times, must be regarded as illustrations of the *human condition.* The historical occasion on which a particular verse was revealed and of the historical description of earlier times, must be utilised in order to extract the underlying purport of that verse and its inner relevance to the ethical teachings which the Qur'ān, taken as a whole, propounds.

In its final compilation, the Qur'ān is arranged in accordance with the inner requirements of its Message as a whole, and not in the chronological order in which the individual chapters (*sūrahs*) or passages were revealed.

The Qur'ān: Its Own Best Commentary

The Qur'ān must not be viewed as a compilation of individual injunctions and exhortations but as *one integral whole.* It is an exposition of an ethical doctrine in which every verse and sentence has an intimate bearing on other verses and sentences, all of them clarifying and amplifying one another.

Consequently the real meaning of the Qur'ān can be grasped only if we group and correlate every one of its statements with what has been stated elsewhere in its pages, and try to explain its ideas by means of frequent cross-references, always subordinating the particular to the general.

3.2 The Purpose of the Qur'ān

Divine writs were also given to other Prophets, but only four: the Torah, the Psalms, the Gospel (*Injīl*) and the Qur'ān, are mentioned by name in the Qur'ān:

> *It was to them that We vouchsafed revelation, and sent judges and prophethood. And now, although the unbelievers may choose to deny these truths* (know that) We have entrusted them to people who will never fail to acknowledge them.*
>
> (Al-An'ām, 6: 89)

> *Step by step has He bestowed upon you from on High His divine writ, setting forth the Truth which confirms whatever there still remains (of earlier revelations): for it is He Who has bestowed from on High the Torah and*

* The manifestation of the Oneness of Allah and the Revelation of His will through the Prophets.

the Injīl aforetime; as a guidance to mankind, and it is He Who has bestowed (upon man) the standard by which to distinguish the true from the false.

(Āl 'Imrān, 3: 3–4)

We have inspired you (O Prophet) as We inspired Noah and all the prophets after him – as We inspired Abraham and Ismael, and Isaac, and Jacob, and their descendants, including Jesus and Job and Jonah, and Aaron and Solomon; and as We vouchsafed unto David the Psalms (Zabūr).

(An-Nisā', 4: 163)

The Qur'ān preaches the same way of life which was preached by all previous Prophets.

(And as for you, O Prophet) nothing is being said to you that has not been said to all (of Allah's) Messengers before you.

Behold, your Sustainer is indeed full of forgiveness but He has also the power to requisite most grievously.

(Fuṣṣilat, 41: 43)

Ibrāhīm was neither Jew nor Christian. He was an upright man, one who had surrendered himself to Allah. He was no polytheist.

Surely the persons who are nearest to Ibrāhīm are those who follow him, this Prophet, and the true believers. Allah is the guardian of the faithful.

(Āl 'Imrān, 3: 67–8)

We have sent forth other Messengers before you and given them wives and children. And none of them could work miracles except by Allah's leave.

Every age has had its revelation. Allah confirms or abolishes what He pleases. With Him is the Mother Book.

(Ar-Ra'd, 13: 38–9)

> *For (even) before you, (O Muḥammad) We never sent (as Our Messengers) any but (mortal) men whom We inspired. However, (tell the deviants of the Truth): 'If you do not know this, ask the followers of earlier revelation.' Nor did We give them bodies that ate no food, nor were they immortal.*
>
> (Al-Anbiyā', 21: 7–8)

> *He has ordained for you the faith which He enjoined on Nūḥ and which We have revealed to you and which We enjoined on Ibrāhīm, Mūsā and 'Īsā, saying: 'Observe the faith and be not divided therein.' Hard for the polytheists is that to which you call them. Allah chooses to Himself whom He wills, and guides to Himself those who turn to Him.*
>
> (Ash-Shūrā, 42: 13)

The Messengers of Allah in essence have been the same throughout all ages.

The Qur'ān is the Fundamental Law of human life in that it provides a Complete Code of Guidance in all spiritual as well as material requirements. Hence the only way to satisfy human life and achieve its overall success is to follow completely, and with absolute certainty the Guidance which the Qur'ān has provided. The purpose of the Qur'ān, therefore, was to bring man from darkness into light, to expose what was concealed by evil and teach the Truth.

> *He has revealed to you this divine writ with the Truth, confirming what preceded it; and He has already revealed the Torah and the Gospel as a guidance unto mankind; and it is He Who has bestowed (upon man) the standard by which to discern the Truth from the false.*
>
> (Āl 'Imrān, 3: 3–4)

> *O People of the Book! Now there has come unto you Our Messenger, to make clear unto you much of what you have been concealing (from yourselves) of the Book, and to forgive you much.*

> *Now there has come unto you from Allah a light, and a clear divine writ, through which Allah shows unto all that seek His goodly acceptance the paths leading to salvation and, by His Grace, brings them out of the depth of darkness into the light and guides them onto a Straight Path.*
>
> (Al-Mā'idah, 5: 15–16)

> *Alif Lām Rā. We have revealed unto you this divine writ so that, by the will of their Sustainer, you may lead people from darkness to light, to the path of the Mighty Glorious One: the path of Allah; Allah to Whom belongs all that is in the heavens and on the earth.*
>
> (Ibrāhīm, 14: 1–2)

> *Whereas those who have attained to faith and do righteous deeds and have come to believe in what has been revealed to Muḥammad – for it is the truth from their Sustainer. Allah will efface their (past) bad deeds, and will set their hearts at rest.*
>
> (Muḥammad, 47: 2)

> *It is He Who has sent forth among the unlettered a Messenger of their own to recite to them His revelations, to purify them, and to instruct them in the Book and wisdom, though they had been hitherto in gross error.*
>
> (Al-Jumu'ah, 62: 2)

The main purpose of the Qur'ān is to revive and make acceptable the Message of Allah which, though precisely sent through earlier Prophets, was changed, modified, forgotten, concealed and mixed up with *Kufr* and *Shirk* by the descendants of Banī Isrā'īl:

> *Behold, it is We Ourselves Who have bestowed from on high, step by step, this reminder: and, behold, it is We Who shall truly guard it (from all corruption).*
>
> (Al-Ḥijr, 15: 9)

For behold, it is for Us to gather it (in your heart) and the reciting of it (as it ought to be read).

(Al-Qiyāmah, 75: 17)

So human beings should follow it with full faith and conviction in its authenticity, its origin, and achieve the success of life in this world as well as in the Next.

The first objective of the Qur'ān is to bring the relationship of man to Allah under the direct Command of Allah. Its second objective is to establish the relationship of man to man strictly according to Allah's Commandments.

3.3 *Tawḥīd* – The Oneness of Allah

Say: 'He is Allah, the One and Only. Allah the Eternal, the Independent. Neither has He an offspring nor is He the offspring of anyone: and none is equal with Him in rank.'

(Al-Ikhlāṣ, 112: 1–4)

The Prophet (peace be upon him) described this short *sūrah* as equivalent to one-third of the whole of the Qur'ān. Scholars have cited many reasons for this. The most plausible one being that of the three basic tenets of Islam – *Tawḥīd, Ākhirah* and *Risālah*, this *sūrah* sums up the concept of *Tawḥīd* exactly and precisely. This *sūrah* was recited by the Prophet (peace be upon him) firstly in Makkah and two or three times in Madinah whenever the opponents of Islam raised objections and asked questions about Allah. Basically this *sūrah* is Makkan (revealed in Makkah) but some consider it Madinan as it was also recited in Madinah.

The idea of the oneness of Allah and His uniqueness is expressed in the Qur'ān several times in varying formulations.

Allah is but One God; hallowed be He that there should be unto Him a son! Unto Him belongs all that is in the heavens and all that is on earth. And Allah is the All-Sufficient Protector.

(An-Nisā', 4: 171)

Oh, verily, it is out of their own falsehood that some people assert, 'Allah has begotten (sons and daughters).' Surely they lie.

(Aṣ-Ṣāffāt, 37: 151–2)

And yet, they attribute to some of His Servants a share with Him. Surely man is manifestly ungrateful.

(Az-Zukhruf, 43: 15)

He is the Originator of the heavens and the earth. How could He have a son when He has no consort. And it is He Who has created everything, and He alone knows everything.

(Al-An'ām, 6: 101)

They say: 'The Most Gracious has taken unto Himself a son.' Glory be to Allah; Nay, they (whom they describe as His offspring) are but honoured servants. They do not speak till He has spoken; they act by His command. He knows what is before them and behind them. They intercede for none save those whom He accepts, and tremble in awe of Him. Whoever declares: 'I am a god besides Him' shall be requited with Hell-fire. Thus We reward the wrong-doers.

(Al-Anbiyā', 21: 26–9)

They assert: 'Allah has taken unto Himself a son!' Glory be to Allah; Self-Sufficient is He: unto Him belongs all that is in the heavens and all that is on earth! No evidence whatever have you for this (assertion)! Would you ascribe unto Allah something of which you have no knowledge?

(Yūnus, 10: 68)

And say: 'All praise is due to Allah, Who begets no offspring, and has no partner in His Sovereignty, and has no weakness; who needs none to defend Him from humiliation.' And extol His limitless Greatness.

(Al-Isrā', 17: 111)

Sūrah al-Ikhlāṣ (112) in the first four short sentences answers all the questions about God. First, the declaration about Allah concerns His characteristic of being *aḥad*. The Prophet (peace be upon him) is asked to say: *'My Lord Whom you want to know is none but Allah.' It is the same Being you know by the name of Allah.*

'Allah' was not an unfamiliar word for the Arabs in the pre-Islamic era. They had been using this very word for the Creator of the universe since the earliest times. For other gods they used the word *ilāh*. They knew in their heart of hearts that no *ilāh* could help them on any critical occasion except Allah. The polytheistic Arabs' belief about Allah is expressed in the Qur'ān in many places:

Yet if you ask them who created them, they will promptly reply that it was Allah. How can they turn away from Him?

(Az-Zukhruf, 43: 87)

If you ask them who it is who created the heavens and the earth and subjected the sun and the moon, they will say: 'Allah'. How then can they turn away from Him?

(Al-'Ankabūt, 29: 61)

Say: 'Who provides for you from heaven and earth? Who has endowed you with hearing and sight? Who brings forth the living from the dead, and the dead from the living? Who ordains all things?' They will reply: 'Allah'.

(Yūnus, 10: 31)

When at sea a misfortune befalls you, all but He of those to whom you pray forsake you; yet when He brings you safe to dry land, you turn your backs upon Him. Truly, man is ever thankless.

(Al-Isrā', 17: 67)

Say: 'Whose is the earth and all that it contains? (Tell me) if you know the Truth.'

'Allah's', they reply.

Say: 'Then will you not take heed?'

Say: 'Who is the Lord of the seven heavens, and of the Glorious Throne?'

'Allah', they will reply.

Say: 'Will you not keep from evil, then?'

Say: 'In whose hands is the Sovereignty of all things, protecting all, while against Him there is no protection? Tell me if you know the truth.'

'In Allah's', they will reply.

Say: 'How then can you be so bewitched?'

(Al-Mu'minūn, 23: 84–9)

The first verse of *Sūrah al-Ikhlāṣ, Qul Huwallāhu Aḥad,* is a very comprehensive expression. About Allah it conveys the following concepts:

1. He alone is the Sustainer; no one else has any share or part in providence, and since He alone is the *Ilāh* (deity) Who is the Master and Sustainer, therefore no one else is His associate in Divinity either.
2. He alone is the Creator of the universe; no one else is His associate in the whole of creation. He alone is the Master of the universe, the Dispenser and Administrator of its system, the Sustainer of His creations, Helper and Rescuer in times of hardship; no one else has any share or part whatever in divinity which belongs exclusively to Allah.

3. He alone has been, and will be, God for ever; neither was there a god before Him, nor will there be any after Him.

The attribute *Aḥad* is not used for anyone except Allah for He alone is the Being Who exists without any plurality in any way, Whose Oneness is perfect in every way.

The second unique characteristic of Allah (*swt*) is His being *Aṣ-Ṣamad.* One thing to be noted here is that the words are *Allāh-uṣ-Ṣamad* and not *Allāh Ṣamad.* As *ṣamad* can also be used for creatures, *Aṣ-Ṣamad* signifies that the real and true *ṣamad* is Allah alone.

The third verse totally negates the concept of sonship or fathership *vis-à-vis* Allah. The polytheists held the concept that like human beings, gods also belong to a species which has many members who marry, beget and are begotten. Thus arises the question of the ancestry of Allah, a notion about which the Prophet (peace be upon him) was questioned.

To strengthen and support the two attributes of *Aḥad* and *Aṣ-Ṣamad* the third verse, 'Neither has He an offspring nor is He the offspring of another', leaves no room for any ambiguity in this regard.

The last verse, 'None is equal with Him in rank', logically correlates to the Oneness and Uniqueness of Allah, without beginning and without end.

Thus the quality of His Being is beyond the range of human comprehension and imagination. Any attempt to 'depict' Allah by means of figurative representations or even abstract symbols must be branded as blasphemous denials of the Truth.

The attribution of 'sonship' to God either in a real or metaphorical sense presupposes a degree of inherent likeness between the 'father' and the 'son'. In Islam, Allah is unique in every respect, so that:

> *. . . there is nothing like unto Him, and He alone is All-Hearing, All-Seeing.*
>
> (Ash-Shūrā, 42: 11)

The concept of 'progeny' implies an organic continuation of the progenitor in another being. It presupposes a degree of incompleteness before the act of procreation or incarnation.

Even if the idea of 'sonship' is expressed only as one of the different 'aspects' of the One Deity (as in the 'Trinity' of Christianity), the Qur'ān considers it blasphemous because it amounts to an attempt to define Allah Who is 'Sublimely exalted above anything that man may devise by way of definition.'

> *That men should ascribe a son to the Most Gracious although it is inconceivable that the Most Gracious should take unto Himself a son.*
>
> (Maryam, 19: 91–2)

Tawḥīd is the backbone of Islam. This very clear belief in Allah can set human beings on the right track. This was the reason that the Prophet (peace be upon him) did not accept any compromise with the Quraysh (pagan Arabs) for undermining the pure concept of the Oneness of Allah as revealed in the Qur'ān.

It is quite obvious from the Qur'ān and the dealings of the Prophet (peace be upon him) that Islam strongly demands that mankind should always be conscious of the Creator's Oneness and any deviation from this concept of *Tawḥīd* is an unforgivable sin.

Tawḥīd is not so much for the recognition of Allah's Oneness by man as Allah is self-sufficient and there are angels and other creatures that always acknowledge the Oneness of Allah. The only reason for making the cognition of *Tawḥīd* as the cardinal, the supreme postulate in His final Message to humanity is that it is essential for humanity's benefit.

Tawḥīd – Its Benefits for Humanity

1. To free man from superstitious feelings of dependence on all sorts of imaginary powers or forces of nature. To provide dignity and freedom from all manner of superstitions by creating a consciousness of being responsible to none except Allah – the Ultimate Reality.
2. To bring home to man that he depends extensively on, and is responsible to, the One and only Power.
3. Considering the Omnipresence, Omniscience and All-Embracing Wisdom of Allah, man can be sure that at the moment of Judgement not only his outward actions but also his innermost feelings and urges will justly, and without any arbitrariness, be taken into account by Allah (*swt*) Who has created man as he is: a frail being always in need of Divine Guidance.
4. The concept of *Tawḥīd*, the Oneness of Allah, logically demands that His Oneness must be reflected in the unity of His creation as well. This means to have a unity of purpose underlying Divine creation. Hence everything in the universe, whether concrete or abstract, is meaningful and not 'accidental'.
5. The purpose of the creation by Allah alone leads to the idea that there is no inherent contradiction between the various manifestations of creation. There is rather some inherent wisdom in any apparent contradictions.
6. Harmony in the universe demands that there should be no inherent conflict between the physical and spiritual elements of human life. The needs of the spirit and the urges of the body must be coordinated and

harmonised by man's moral will in such a way that the coherent integral permeability of the human being reflects the Creator's Oneness.

7. In order to completely avoid any contradiction about the Oneness of Allah, man's social life should as a corollary also be capable of harmonisation such that there are no conflicts and tensions among the individual members. This directs us away from the concept of one individual as being superior to another by virtue of his birth or social function.

Conclusion

Allah (*swt*), by declaring and repeatedly stressing His Own Oneness and Uniqueness, confers a three-fold benefit on humanity:

1. Peace with Allah

Allah bestows upon human beings freedom and spiritual dignity by providing the conviction that all creation, including human life, is not the outcome of a play of blind forces, but rather has a definite meaning and a definite purpose. Thus, man attains peace with his own destiny and with Allah.

2. Peace with himself

Man is informed through the Oneness of Allah that there is no inherent contradiction between the physical and the spiritual aspects of his own life. Thus, he may achieve peace within himself.

3. Peace with his social environment and his fellow men

One person is superior to another, not by birth or social function, but by virtue alone. Efforts to achieve social justice should take guidance and inspiration from the absolute transcendental justice inherent in the unique wisdom of Allah.

Hence our social life, as well as our individual life, must be subordinated to the principle of moderation and equity, a just balance between what is due and necessary to oneself and what is due to others.

3.4 *Ākhirah* – The Life Hereafter

> *Alif. Lām. Mīm.*
> *Defeated are the Byzantines in the lands close-by; yet it is they who, notwithstanding this their defeat, shall be victorious within a few years: (for) with Allah rests all power of decision, before and after.*
>
> *And on that day the believers (too) will rejoice in Allah's succour. He grants victory to whom He wills, since He alone is Almighty, the Merciful.*
>
> (Ar-Rūm, 30: 1–5)

Sūrah Ar-Rūm (The Byzantines) opens with the prophecy about the Byzantines (Romans). It is a very interesting and eye-opening declaration revealed by Allah some six years before the *Hijrah* (migration to Madinah) and eight years before the fulfilment of the prophecy. It was revealed in the year in which the migration to Habashah (Abyssinia) took place.

The defeats and victories mentioned above are related to the last phases of the centuries-long struggle between the Byzantine and Persian Empires. The verse first mentions the event that took place at the time of its revelation. At that time, in the Byzantine-occupied territories adjacent to Arabia, i.e. Jordan, Syria and Palestine, the Romans were completely overpowered by the Persians in 615 CE (corresponding to six years before the *Hijrah*). Thus the total destruction of the Byzantine Empire seemed imminent.

The Muslims around the Prophet (peace be upon him) were frustrated at hearing the news of the Byzantine's defeat. They were, after all, Christians who believed as such in the One God while the pagan Quraysh sympathised with the Persians who, according to the Quraysh, opposed the concept of One God.

The above verses then declared two prophecies: first, the Romans would be victorious and second, the Muslims would also gain a victory 'within a few years'. The Arabic term *biḍ' 'sinīn* denotes any number between three and ten years.

When these verses were revealed, the disbelievers of Makkah ridiculed Muslims because, apparently, there was not a remote chance of the fulfilment of either prediction in a few years. In 622 CE, six years after the revelation of the above verses, as the Prophet (peace be upon him) migrated to Madinah, Emperor Heraclius of Byzantine succeeded in defeating the Persians at Issus, south of the Taurus Mountains and subsequently driving them out of Asia Minor. In 624 CE, Heraclius entered Azerbaijan and destroyed Clorumia, the birth-place of Zoroaster, and ravaged the principal fire-temple of Iran. This was eight years after the revelation of the verses, when the Muslims achieved a decisive victory at Badr for the first time against the Makkan polytheists. Thus both predictions made in these verses were fulfilled simultaneously within the stipulated period of under ten years.

The predictions made in these verses offer the most outstanding evidence of the Qur'ān being the Word of Allah and the Prophet Muḥammad (peace be upon him) being His true Messenger. At the end, Allah makes it clear that the victories of both the Byzantines and the Muslims were achieved because of His support and will. This support or help is coupled with His Justice. Allah is Powerful as well as Merciful. Out of His Mercy, He takes care of the oppressed because they are relatively better in conduct and belief than their opponents.

Then, following these two unequivocal predictions the direction of the discourse turns to the central theme of the Hereafter.

> *(This is) Allah's promise. Never does Allah fail to fulfil His promise – but most people know (it) not. They know*

but the outward aspect of this world's life, whereas of the Hereafter they are heedless.

(Ar-Rūm, 30: 6–7)

Man is accustomed to seeing only what is apparent and superficial. That which is behind the apparent and superficial he does not know. So just by relying on apparent and superficial manifestations man can make wrong estimates and this because of his lack of knowledge about the future.

This leads to the Hereafter. There are plenty of Signs and evidence which point to the Hereafter but people are heedless of these due to their own short-sightedness. They only see the apparent and outward aspect of this worldly life and are unaware of what is hidden behind it.

Have they not reflected on their own selves?

(Ar-Rūm, 30: 8)

It follows that if people reflect on their own selves, apart from the external phenomena, they will realise the necessity of a second life after the present one. The following represent three special characteristics of a human being.

1. All the bounties of the earth and around it are bestowed upon human beings for their use.
2. Man is free to choose a way of life for himself. He can follow virtue or vice, obedience or denial, the way of belief or disbelief.
3. Man judges deeds as good and bad and decides on a good action to be rewarded and an evil one to be punished.

These three characteristics in themselves identify that man will be called to account for his deeds, for the use of the powers delegated to him. This call will happen after man's life-activity has finished. The checking and auditing of the account will be done only after all the activities of not only one man, or one nation but of all mankind living in this world have expired. Hence, the very pattern of living in this world demands that after the present life there will be another life when a court will be established, the life-record of every person be examined justly and then reward or punishment be given according to one's deeds.

> *Allah has not created the heavens and the earth and all that is between them without (an inner) Truth and a term set (by Him). And yet, behold, there are many people who (stubbornly) deny (the Truth) that they are destined to meet their Sustainer.*
>
> (Ar-Rūm, 30: 8)

Two further arguments are advanced for the Hereafter in the above passage.

1. The universe has been created purposively. It is a well-organised system in which every component testifies that it has been created with great wisdom. Every phenomenon is governed by a law, the discovery of which has enabled man to design his social and economic living. This indicates that the Almighty, the Wise Being, must have a purpose and a scheme in creating this world and assigning the affairs as He has to His creation, to human beings, endowed with great mental and physical capabilities, power and authority, and freedom of action and choice.

   So, is it possible and logical that the whole record of man's life-activity will be just set aside after his death without any accountability? Hence, justice demands that there should be another life in which man has to live according to the performance of his deeds in this world. That world will be the world where he receives reward or punishment.

2. A close observation of the system of the universe indicates that everything in this world has an age

appointed for it after which it dies and expires. Nothing here is immortal. All the forces working in the universe are limited and the universe too, will expire as a whole. Science also identifies that matter and energy are changeable and non-persistent. The second law of thermodynamics states that there is a decrease in entropy and the material world has neither existed since eternity nor will it last till eternity. This again proves the occurrence of resurrection.

And have they never travelled in the earth and beheld what was the fate of their forebears. Far mightier were they; they tilled the land and built more on it than they have built. Their Messengers came to them with Clear Signs. Allah did not wrong them, but they wronged themselves. Evil was the end of the evil-doers, because they denied the revelations of Allah and scoffed at them.

(Ar-Rūm, 30: 9–10)

In these verses, a historical agument is presented for the Hereafter. It is claimed that denial of the Hereafter is not a new phenomenon and that a large number of people, sometimes entire nations, denied it altogether or lived without caring for their accountability after death. History shows that any form of denial or non-realisation of the Hereafter resulted in the corruption and immorality of the people. The experience of history proves that denial of the reality of the Hereafter is fatal to mankind.

Many regard material progress as the sign of a nation following the Right Path. Here the Qur'ān rejects this notion. It is made clear that the mere material progress of a people lacking in right belief and conduct is not going to save them from becoming the fuel of Hell.

On the one hand, there are evidences in man's own self, in the universe around him, and the continuous experience of human history; and on the other, there have also been the

Prophets (peace be upon them), one after the other, who showed clear signs, as a proof of their being true Prophets and also warned people that the Hereafter is sure to come.

Persons or nations that neither think rightly themselves nor adopt the right attitude by listening to others will be in the end themselves responsible for their destruction. Allah will not be unjust to them for they have been unjust to themselves by not following the directions and guidance given by the Prophets of their times.

> *Allah brings His creation into being and then He reproduces them. To Him He will recall you all.*
>
> *And when the Last Hour dawns, the wrong-doers will be speechless with despair. None of their partners will intercede for them; indeed they shall even disown their associates.*
>
> *And when the Last Hour dawns, (mankind) will be separated one from the other. Those who have believed and done good works shall rejoice in a Garden and those who have disbelieved and denied Our Revelations and the meeting of the life to come, shall be delivered up for punishment.*
>
> (Ar-Rūm, 30: 11–16)

It seems easy for man to believe that God is the Creator but it becomes a little difficult to believe that God will bring dead human beings back to life. Scientifically, reproduction or recreation should be an easier process than original production or creation. But in the case of God it depends entirely upon the concept of God in one's mind. If we believe in this true attribute of God, then without any hesitation, we will believe that God can recreate or reproduce His creations at any time, at any moment.

The wrong-doers mentioned here are not just those who have committed murder, robbery and rape in this world but include all those who have rebelled against God, denied the accountability of the Hereafter and who have worshipped others than Allah, or their own selves. When such people come back to life in the Hereafter, against their expectations, they will be dumbfounded.

There are three kinds of associates mentioned here:

1. The angels, prophets, saints, martyrs and righteous people, to whom the polytheists assign Divine attributes and powers and whom they worship as gods, constitute the first category. On Resurrection Day these persons will rebuke their worshippers, they will say that they were made associates by the worshippers without their consent and against their teachings. Hence, these alleged associates will declare their complete dissociation from their worshippers.
2. Inanimate things, such as the moon, the sun, the planets, trees and stones which are worshipped as gods by the polytheists, form the second group. These are helpless things and will not be able to say anything on their behalf or against them.
3. The arch-criminals, e.g. Satan, false religious guides, tyrants and despots, who by deception and fraud or who by use of force compelled God's servants to worship them, belong to the third category. They themselves will be in trouble on the Day of Resurrection. Unable to intercede for others, they will rather try to prove before Allah that their worshippers and followers were themselves responsible for their evil-doings and therefore their deviation should not be credited to their account.

In this way, then, the polytheists will not enjoy any intercession from anywhere. They will themselves admit their mistake of making associates with Allah. In the Hereafter the polytheists will disown the polytheism (*shirk*) which misled them in this world.

On Resurrection Day the groupings of mankind will be different from those in this world. Instead of groups based on race, country, language, tribe and clan, economic and political interests, mankind will be regrouped on the basis of true belief, morality and character. According to Islam, the real differentiation for mankind is belief and morality.

It is important to note that good works are mentioned as a necessary adjunct of the faith. In order to enter Paradise, belief is not enough but good works should be the spontaneous outcome of true belief.

> *Therefore, glorify Allah when you enter the evening and when you rise in the morning. Praise be to Him in the heavens and the earth, in the afternoon and at the declining of the day.*
>
> (Ar-Rūm, 30: 17–18)

This order was given to the Prophet (peace be upon him) and through him to all the Believers. The disbelievers, by denying the life Hereafter regard Allah as someone helpless. As opposed to them, the Prophet (peace be upon him) and the Believers glorify Allah and proclaim that He is free from and exalted above defects, faults and weaknesses.

The best form of such proclamation and expression is the five-times-a-day prescribed Prayers. These verses clearly point to the times of the *Fajr* (morning), *Maghrib* (evening), *'Aṣr* (declining of the day) and *Ẓuhr* (afternoon) Prayers. Furthermore, the following verses of the Qur'ān point to the time of Prayers.

> *Establish the ṣalāt from the declining of the sun to the darkness of the night, and be particular about the recital of the Qur'ān at dawn.*
>
> (Al-Isrā', 17: 78)

> *Establish the ṣalāt at the two ends of the day and in the early parts of the night.*
>
> (Hūd, 11: 114)

> *And glorify your Sustainer with His praise before the rising of the sun and before its setting, and glorify Him again during the hours of the night and at the extremes of the day.*
>
> (Ṭa Hā, 20: 130)

Allah is ever bringing into existence countless animals and human beings by breathing life into dead matter. You witness the phenomenon of lands which lie barren and then on receiving water begin to blossom and flourish. Life and death are both controlled by Allah.

From here onward in this *sūrah*, in verses 20 to 27, the Signs of Allah are mentioned. These Signs, on the one hand, point towards the possibility and occurrence of the life Hereafter as mentioned in the above verses. On the other, the same Signs also underscore that this universe is under One God alone, the Creator, Master and Ruler. Thus the two beliefs, Resurrection (*Ākhirah*) and the Oneness of God (*Tawḥīd*) are intertwined.

> *And of His Signs is that He created you out of dust – and then, lo! you become human beings scattered far and wide!*
>
> (Ar-Rūm, 30: 20)

Man has been created out of a few dead elements such as carbon, calcium and the like. A unique creation, man has great powers of sentiment, consciousness, initiative, and choice. Not only was one man created but to him and his partner wonderful procreative powers were given by Allah by means of which billions of human beings have been reproduced. This poses some very serious questions.

First, could this unique creation have come into existence without the design and creative power of a Wise Creator? Second, could this creation be the result of the thinking and design of many gods or just One God? Third, given that the One God Who brought man into being from absolute nothingness, is it not also the case that He can bring man back to life after giving death? The only answer to all these questions is that life and death are controlled by the One and only Allah. For Him the transfer from life to death or death to life is trivial, easy.

> *And of His Signs is that He created for you mates out of your own kind, so that you might live in tranquillity with them. And He engendered love and kindness between you. In this behold, there are messages indeed for people who think.*
>
> (Ar-Rūm, 30: 21)

In this verse another Sign of Allah's wisdom is depicted. He has created mankind in two sexes – male and female. Both are identical in humanity having the same figure and form but differing in their bio-sexual performance. There is such a wonderful harmony between the two that each is a perfect counterpart of the other. The following represent those inferences that can be drawn from this phenomenon.

1. It clearly indicates that Allah has created everything in this universe in pairs. Each entity needs its pair for its completion. Hence, this material world also has its pair, known as the Hereafter. Worldly life achieves fulfilment by Life-after-Death as its complement.
2. Allah has engrained sexual attraction between a male and female. This sexual love makes a pair work and live together with full confidence and reliability.
3. The pairs differ from each other but Allah the Creator and Sustainer arranges for a deep coordination between the two.

> *And of His Signs are the creation of the heavens and the earth and the diversity of your tongues and colours. In this, behold, there are messages indeed for the learned.*
>
> (Ar-Rūm, 30: 22)

In this verse two more Signs are mentioned: the creation of the heavens and the earth and the diversity of mankind's tongues and colours.

When one reflects on the origin of the initial energy that assumed the form of matter with its combination of elements to create an awe-inspiring universal system and then further reflects on the functioning of this system for many millions of years with its precise regularity and discipline, one can only conclude that this could not have happened by mere chance, that it is the work of the All-Embracing Will and Command of the All-Knowing, All-Wise Creator.

Attention is drawn here to only two aspects of diversity, namely, speech and colour, but if one looks around, one will find countless different species of man, animal, plant and the like. Even two leaves of a tree are not exactly alike. Anyone who observes this wonderful phenomenon with open eyes can only conclude that the Maker of the universe is ever-engaged in His creative and sustaining activity.

> *And of His Signs is your sleep, at night or day as well as your search for His bounties. In this, behold, there are messages indeed for those who pay heed.*
>
> (Ar-Rūm, 30: 23)

Allah has made day and night for work and sleep respectively. But this is not a hard and fast law. So during both day and night you may sleep as well as work for your livelihood. This Sign identifies that Allah is not only the Creator but is also extremely Compassionate and Merciful in that He arranges for the needs and requirements of His creatures.

Allah has placed a powerful urge for sleep in mankind. Sleep overtakes man and compels him to have a few hours of rest in order to be refreshed.

Man has further been given the appropriate limits and suitable physical and mental capabilities for exploring the means and resources of his livelihood.

> *And of His Signs is that He shows you the lightning (to cause) fear and hope. He sends down water from the skies, giving life thereby to the earth after its death. In this, behold, there are messages indeed for people who use their reason.*
>
> (Ar-Rūm, 30: 24)

Thunder and lightning are associated with rain. This rain is then the cause of hope for the crops to grow as well as the fear that lightning may damage something or prolonged heavy rain may wash the land away.

The creatures of the world live on the products that emanate from the earth. This depends on rain. This rain falls directly on the earth or its water gathers together on the surface of the earth, or freezes on the mountains and then flows down in the form of rivers. Further rain itself depends on the heat of the sun, the change of seasons and atmospheric changes in temperature, and the circulation of the winds, etc.

The harmony and proportion between these different entities existing on our planet for many millions of years clearly shows the All-Embracing Will, Plan and Wisdom of Allah, the Designer.

> *And of His signs is that the skies and the earth stand firm at His bidding.*
>
> *(Remember all this; for) in the end, when He will call you forth from the earth with a single call – lo! you will (all) emerge (for the Judgement).*
>
> *For, unto Him belongs every being that is in the heavens and on earth; all things directly obey His will.*
>
> *And He it is Who creates (all life) in the first instance, and then brings it forth nigh: and most easy is this for Him since His is the essence of all that is most sublime in*

the heavens and on earth, and He alone is Almighty, Truly Wise.

(Ar-Rūm, 30: 25–7)

The heavens and the earth have not only come into being by Allah's Command but their continuous functioning is also due to His Command. He sustains them to stand firm and not collapse.

Enumerating upon all these Signs makes man realise Allah's Power and Authority. As regards the Resurrection, two things are clearly mentioned here. First, Allah will not have to unduly prepare for raising mankind back to life after death. His one call will be enough to raise and muster together from every corner of the earth all human beings. Second, since it was not difficult for Allah to create human beings in the first instance, how can it be difficult for Him to resurrect them again? Reproduction should be easier than production.

The Qur'ān is full of verses directing us towards belief in *Ākhirah*. *Tawḥīd* – the Oneness of Allah and *Ākhirah* – Life-after-Death, are concepts that are essential for living in this world. Without these two doctrines, mankind, individually or collectively, can never attain a lifestyle leading to peace and justice.

3.5 The Achievement of the Qur'ān

The unique Message of the Qur'ān is to invite all mankind towards belief in the Absolute Unity of Allah and the final prophethood of Muḥammad (peace be upon him) through whom Allah the Almighty chose to manifest His Will to mankind, and guide them to the Right Path – the path of ultimate success in this life as well as the Next.

The Qur'ān propounds a two-fold Islamic ideology. First, it requires human beings to live in this universe and make use of things, not according to man's own wishes but according to the Commands of Allah. Second, in all activities of life the ultimate objective must be the Pleasure of Allah, achieved by sacrificing one's own pleasure to His pleasure.

According to the current non-Islamic standard, the main consideration in morality is the acquisition of happiness. This means that the things which give happiness are moral and the things which do not give happiness are immoral. Hence every activity of human life is with a view to gaining happiness in the material sense, even at the cost of the life and property of others. According to the Qur'ānic injunction, the basic consideration should be the Pleasure of Allah. Every act is to be performed with the sole objective of gaining Allah's Pleasure irrespective of its result and, therefore, according to the Qur'an, only that act is rewarding which has been declared as good by Allah the Almighty.

The Qur'ān, during its 23-year period of revelation, practised by the Prophet (peace be upon him) and his Companions (*ra*) revolutionised human society on earth in the form of the Islamic era. So what then are the attributes of Islam?

1. It abolished infidelity and polytheism through the absolute belief in One God – the Creator and Administrator of the entire universe, and exclusive worship of and total submission to Him.

2. It developed fear of accountability among people thus motivating good moral behaviour through belief in the Day of Judgement, Paradise and Hell.

3. It removed the indecencies of human life and created piety and sublimity of character among people through the five-times-a-day compulsory Prayers and the month of fasting every year.

4. It provided a very effective system of keeping wealth in circulation for use by, and the welfare of, the society at large through the system of *Zakāt,* charity, wills, gifts, *waqf,* interest-free loans, etc.

5. It created a unique type of unity in belief and action among its followers and established an international institution for their gathering together, at least once a year through *Ḥajj* and through facing the Ka'bah in Prayers.
6. It rejected the practise of monasticism through establishing and promoting family life.
7. It eradicated vices in human society through justice and equity, respect for life and property, and banning of gambling, adultery, bribery and theft.
8. It uprooted mischief and violence from society and established peace and tranquillity through agreements and treaties with, and well-organised and well-planned war against the enemy on the battlefield.

CHAPTER FOUR

Historical Perspective

4.1 The Purpose of Human Creation

(Recall) when your Sustainer said to the angels, 'I am about to establish upon earth a vicegerent.' They said, 'Will You place on it such as will spread corruption thereon and shed blood, whereas it is we who extol Your Limitless Glory, and praise You, and hallow Your name?'

Allah replied: 'I know that which you do not know.'

And He imparted unto Adam the names of all things. Then He set these before the angels and asked, 'Tell Me the names of these, if what you say is true.'

They replied, 'Glory be to You; we have no knowledge except that which You have given us. Indeed You alone are All-Knowing, Truly Wise.'

Said He, 'O Adam, convey unto them the names of these things.'

And when Adam told them the names of all these things, Allah declared, 'Did I not tell you that I alone know the hidden realities of the heavens and earth. I know what you disclose and what you hide.'

And when We said to the angels, 'Prostrate yourselves

> *before Adam'; they all prostrated themselves except Iblīs who in his pride refused and became an unbeliever.*
>
> *And We said: 'O Adam, you and your wife, both dwell in the Garden and eat freely thereof whatever you may wish but do not go near this tree, otherwise you shall become wrong-doers.'*
>
> *But Satan made them slip from it and caused them to depart from that in which they had been.*
>
> *And We decreed: 'Now, go down all of you from here. You are enemies of one another. Henceforth you shall dwell and provide for yourselves on the earth for a specified period.'*
>
> *Thereupon Adam received words (of guidance) from his Sustainer, and He accepted his repentance: for indeed He alone is the Acceptor of Repentance, the Dispenser of Grace.*
>
> *We said, 'Now go down, all of you from here. Henceforth there shall come to you guidance from Me now and again: whoever will follow it shall have neither fear nor sorrow, and whoever will refuse to accept it and defy Our revelation, they are destined for the fire, and therein shall they abide.'*
>
> (Al-Baqarah, 2: 30–9)

The Qur'ān, in these verses, throws light on the most important event of human history, the emergence of the first man. The Qur'ān, being the Word of Allah, provides the most authentic knowledge. This knowledge enlightens us not only about the creation of man but also about the purpose of human creation being of much more substance than scientific speculation about man's evolution.

The term *Khalīfah* denotes a person who administers on behalf of some higher authority. Allah entrusted the right of the control and administration of the earth to mankind on His behalf.

> *For, He it is Who has made you administrators on the earth, and has raised some of you by degrees above others, so that He might try you by means of what He has bestowed upon you.*
>
> (Al-An 'ām, 6: 165)

> *Who is it that responds to the distressed when he calls out to Him, and who removes the ill (that caused the distress), and has made you vicegerents on the earth.*
>
> (An-Naml, 27: 62)

> *It is He Who made you vicegerents on the earth. One who denies Him shall bear the burden of his disbelief. In denying Him the unbelievers increase nothing for themselves except odium in the sight of Allah; and this unbelief increases nothing but their perdition.*
>
> (Al-Fāṭir, 35: 39)

The angels do not have initiative and the power of decision-making, though they are holy and pure and are endowed with power by Allah. The angels in their limited vision saw only the mischief consequent from the misuse of man's emotional nature. The angels, not because of jealousy, but because of lack of emotion and analytical capability, did not understand the nature of Allah and His plan. They did not realise what attributes and characteristics are required for a person to act as a vicegerent on earth. The powers of will or choosing and decision-making are essential if one is to act as vicegerent.

The literal translation is that 'Allah taught Adam the names of things'. The word *ism* (name) implies the inner nature, qualities and knowledge of things. It also includes the concepts of entities as well as feelings. Hence, in broad terms, it points towards man's faculty of logical definition and, thus, of conceptual thinking. The particular knowledge, characteristics and feelings which were not bestowed on the angels were conferred upon man by Allah. Mankind thus became able to plan and initiate the administration on earth.

By 'Adam' the whole human race is meant here, just as the angels, when identifying the characteristic of 'spreading corruption on earth and shedding blood' also referred to the whole of mankind.

Literally, *Iblīs* is the one who is frustrated and extremely desperate. This is the name given to the *jinn* who disobeyed Allah and refused to prostrate before Adam as a token of submission to him and his children. Moreover, he requested Allah to grant him the opportunity to tempt mankind up to the Last Day. He is also called Satan. *Iblīs* was not an angel as is commonly held but rather one of the *jinn* who are of a different species:

> *Remember: When We said to the angels, 'Prostrate before Adam', they prostrated but Iblīs did not. He was one of the jinn, so he chose the way of disobedience to his Lord's Commands.*
>
> (Al-Kahf, 18: 50)

It was possible for *Iblīs* to disobey Allah because of his being a *jinn* and not an angel. Angels are Allah's creations that are employed by Allah for the administration of His Kingdom. They do not have any choice or initiative but to obey Allah in all circumstances. The *jinn*, like human beings, have been given the freedom of choice and action.

Satan is not a distinct creature. Those among the *jinn* and human beings who disobey Allah, join the group of *Iblīs* and his followers. Allah lets such persist in their rebellion against Him.

The Status of Vicegerency

In the above-quoted verses, Allah *(swt)* informs us about the creation of life and the universe. Then He states that all things on earth and below are created for the use of human beings. Now in these verses Allah mentions the vicegerency of Adam: Allah handed over the administration of the world to mankind and bestowed upon him the knowledge and insight required for administering the world.

After the description of the event of vicegerency, the story of Banī Isrā'īl is narrated in the next verses. Basically, how vicegerency was handed over to them and then taken away for their not fulfilling their commitments properly. Now this vicegerency has been given to the Muslim *Ummah* who is asked to fulfil and perform this duty.

It is the Will of Allah that all affairs pertaining to the earth be handed over to Adam and his children so that they can make changes and innovations to control and use this world according to the orders and directives of Allah. The necessary intellectual and physical faculties are granted to mankind in order that he perform the duty of vicegerency in the best manner. In addition to the duty of servitude, this vicegerency is a great favour and trust upon mankind. It is also a declaration of the highest status of humanity in this vast universe.

The Elevated Status of Mankind

The prostration to mankind by the angels is an indication of the supremacy of human beings over the angels. The reason for this supremacy is that mankind has been given intellect and wisdom to appreciate the greatness of Allah (*swt*). Man has been given free-will and choice to follow either the right or wrong way of living. Mankind, by committing itself to fulfil the duty of vicegerency with full enthusiasm and capability, proved itself able to bear the burden of Allah's trust. It is also a commitment to follow the directives of Allah in all spheres of life.

The Forbidden Tree

This tree was a trial of abstinence. Since will and determination cannot be ascertained until one has proved the practise of abstinence, will and determination are the only distinctions between humans and animals.

When Adam made the mistake of approaching the forbidden tree, Allah made the decision to have him and Eve thrown out of Paradise and sent down to earth. Actually it was planned that the struggle between right and wrong should be carried out on earth. Another unique milestone was that Adam asked for repentance from Allah which was granted by Him because of His Benevolence.

As Adam was created for life on earth, why was this scene enacted in Paradise? This experience in heaven was a kind of preparation for Adam so that he knew how to use the faculties bestowed upon him. It was done to make Adam alert to temptation, become acquainted with error, and learn to ask for Allah's repentance and forgiveness. Temptation by Satan, the realisation of mistakes, asking for forgiveness and the acceptance of forgiveness by Allah is the cycle that every human being has to face in this world. This story then is a reminder to the whole of mankind.

According to Islam, sovereignty belongs to Allah and vicegerency has been given to mankind. Human beings are not sovereign but are servants of the only Sovereign, Allah. Allah has made mankind the best of His creation, hence mankind is selected by Allah as His best creation.

The Directives of Allah

I – THE POSITION OF MAN

The first reality that clearly emerges from these verses is that man is a vicegerent or deputy of Allah in this world. The following are the characteristics of vicegerency.

1. Man has been given authority in certain domains. It must be kept in mind that Allah, the Omnipotent and Omniscient, has full control and power to carry on the

management of the universe single-handedly. Allah does not need any assistance or contribution. Hence, the purpose of appointing a vicegerent or deputy is nothing else but to put human beings on trial after giving them certain powers and rights. The test is how these discerning powers are used by human beings. Do they use them according to the Will of the Sovereign or independently on their own?

2. Limitations are to be applied on the freedom of the vicegerent. He/she should be clearly informed where to use discerning power, and how to make the decision himself/herself as to what affairs he/she has to conduct within the fixed boundaries. Hence, it is essential to have guidance and injunctions from Allah.
3. A vicegerent cannot, and should not, be left independent, and should not be allowed to carry on his/her activities without any idea of answerability. A vicegerent must be answerable for all his/her deeds and performance. A vicegerent is to be punished for dishonesty and mistakes rendered by him/her and should be rewarded for good performances under the directives of the Sovereign.
4. Vicegerency is open for every human being, but it should be given to, and taken by, the one who fulfils the conditions of vicegerency. The person who carries out the task of vicegerency with full honesty, loyalty and devotion deserves to be called the true vicegerent of Allah while others are traitors and rebels.
5. This assignment is not, by its very nature, individualistic; it is of a social and political nature. All human beings, at least those who believe in this principle of vicegerency, and are willing to accept the role, have to fulfil its duties and requirements individually as well as collectively. For collective pursuit, they have to establish a system to obtain the best results.

6. This vicegerency, that is the administration of the world as God's vicegerent, brings peace and prosperity only when it is carried out according to the directives and the orders of the Sovereign. If a human being, or a group of human beings, manages the affairs of sovereignty according to his/her own idiosyncrasies, neglecting the Will of Allah, it is bound to spread corruption and bloodshed.

II – THE SUPREMACY OF MANKIND

The second reality that comes out of these verses is that mankind is the best of creation to whom the angels were ordered to prostrate before and pay their respects, and *Iblīs* was impeached for not so prostrating to Adam. So, in such a case, it does not behove mankind to worship angels or *jinn* and consider them Allah's partners. The angels and *jinn* are as helpless as human beings in relation to Allah. Whatever knowledge they have, is given by Allah. If Allah so wills, human beings can have much more knowledge than angels. Hence, Allah is the only One to be worshipped. Man degrades himself if he makes angels and *jinn* partners to Allah.

III – THE SOURCE OF EVIL

Man is not a culprit or oppressor by nature. Allah has created him with many talents and capabilities. If he commits a sin, it is because of his abusing his right of autonomy. It is Satan who prompts him to oppress by persuading him to break the few restrictions that Allah has put on man's vast freedom. Satan tells men that these few restrictions are a great hindrance to their comfort and living. Once they are overcome, the doors of progress, comfort and living are open to mankind. Man sees the short-term benefits of these devilish inducements and so becomes trapped. Thus, he indulges in sins against the noble qualities of his nature.

Allah has devised a method of repentance and reform for purifying mankind from these sins. Hence, Allah forgave the sins committed by Adam when he asked for repentance. The coming of Adam to this world was not as a punishment for his sins but a trial to prove himself victorious over Satan and thus to acquire Paradise, his original abode. This statement from the Qur'ān rejects the Christian axiom that Adam is sinful and needs atonement for his salvation.

IV – WISDOM IN EACH DIRECTIVE OF ALLAH

The fourth reality expounded in these verses is that there is deep wisdom and benefit in each and every directive of Allah and these are known only when Allah reveals them. Human beings, angels and *jinn*, none can grasp the real wisdom of Allah's actions. Hence the correct approach for mankind is to make every effort to find wisdom in Allah's directives. He/she should not make objections or grumble when he/she does not understand. He/she should always have the feeling that there is definitely wisdom in a directive from Allah which he/she may not yet have been able to find due to a deficiency in knowledge. This is the correct approach as followed by rightly-guided people.

Those who place the knowledge and wisdom of Allah on the same standard as their limited and partial knowledge, are indulging in the same kind of ego and pride in which *Iblīs* indulged when he refused to prostrate before Adam.

V – THE DIFFERENCE IN THE SINS OF ADAM AND *IBLĪS*

The sin committed because of a weakness in one's will-power is of a different nature from sin committed because of pride and jealousy. There is a good chance of repentance and reform for sins committed due to a weakness of determination. Allah (*swt*) takes care of such persons and guides them on the Right Path. Contrary to this, the disease of those who disobey Allah due to pride and jealousy is a severe one. Instead of being reformed, these people follow their leader *Iblīs*. The sin of Adam was of the first kind and, therefore, he had the courage to ask for repentance which was then granted to him. The sin of *Iblīs* was of the second kind, hence he was deprived of repentance and reform, and ultimately incurred God's curse.

VI – THE NEED FOR GUIDANCE AND PROPHETHOOD

Since Allah has set mankind a hard trial by allowing Satan to mislead him, He, in His Benevolence and Mercy, decided not to leave man to find the Right Path only with the help of his nature and intellect. He also arranged for saving man's intellect from going astray. This could only be fulfilled by the institution of prophethood. In this world of test and trial, the real source of satisfaction and contentment is to be found in the instructions of the Prophets. Once this source of Revelation via the Prophets has vanished, mankind easily becomes the victim of oppression. The void in the nature of mankind can only be filled by following the Prophets' instructions based on Revelation.

4.2 The Purpose of the Creation of Rational Beings

> *And (tell them that) I have not created the Jinn (invisible beings) and human beings to any end other than that they may (know and) worship Me. (But withall), no sustenance do I ever demand of them, nor do I demand that they feed Me: for, verily, Allah Himself is the Provider of all sustenance, the Lord of all Might, the Eternal.*
>
> (Adh-Dhāriyāt, 51: 56–8)

The innermost purpose of the creation of rational beings is their cognition of the existence of Allah, and, hence, their conscious willingness to conform in their own existence to whatever they may perceive of His Will and Plan; and it is this two-fold concept of cognition and willingness that gives the deepest meaning to what the Qur'ān describes as *'Ibādah* (worship). This call for worship does not arise from any supposed 'need' on the part of the Creator, Who is Self-Sufficient and Infinite in His power. This call is designed as an instrument for the inner development of the worshipper, who, by his conscious self-surrender to the All-Pervading Creative Will, may hope to come closer to an understanding of that Will and thus get closer to Allah.

The Message of the Qur'ān to the whole of mankind is explicit and simple:

> *O mankind! Worship your Sustainer, Who has created you and those who lived before you, so that you might remain conscious of Him Who has made the earth a resting place for you and the sky a canopy, and has sent down water from the sky and thereby brought forth fruits for your sustenance. Do not, then, claim that there is any power that could rival Allah, when you know (that He is One).*
>
> (Al-Baqarah, 2: 21–2)

4.3 The Purpose of Revelation

The role of the combined resources of the Divine Message and the human recipients and advocates of that Message has been, from the first Prophet, Adam (*as*), to the last Prophet, Muḥammad (peace be upon him), to change the conduct of human beings in totality.

These Prophets performed the task of propagating the Divine Message. Ibrāhīm (*as*) with his son Ismā'īl (*as*) erected the House of Allah, the Ka'bah at Makkah in the hope that the Commands of Allah would be acted upon by humanity. Of all the Prophets, Mūsā (*as*) was ordained to liberate the Israelites, who were treated badly by the Egyptian Pharaoh. Allah gave the freedom and leadership of the world to Banī Isrā'īl (now known as the Jews). When they failed to maintain the Kingdom of God on earth, Allah chose 'Īsā (Jesus Christ) (*as*) to call them towards the Right Path.

> *And (I have come) to confirm the Truth of whatever there still remains of the Torah and to make lawful to you some of the things which for you are forbidden. I bring you a Sign from your Sustainer. Therefore fear Him and obey me. Allah is my Sustainer and your Sustainer: therefore serve Him. That is the Straight Path.*
>
> (Āl 'Imrān, 3: 50–1)

The Jews, however, refused to mend their ways; hence another group of righteous people, the Christians, the followers of Christ (*as*) came on the world scene. The world was undergoing a tremendous upheaval at the time of the advent of the Qur'ān through Muḥammad (peace be upon him). The old civilisations of Egypt, India, Babylon, Greece and China had been lost. The two great powers, Persia and Rome, controlled the world. Materially, the two civilisations were quite prosperous but moral bankruptcy was at its zenith. These Emperors, with an unholy alliance of religious luminaries and feudal lords, kept humanity in their tyrannical clutches. The masses were treated like animals.

Arabia was also in chaos. The most powerful clan, the Quraysh, was custodian of the Ka'bah, practising paganism and exercising exploitation. The Ka'bah, the House of God, became the centre for idolatrous worship. At this time, the Jews were also exploiting the masses through their intellectual dominance. Usury was a common practice carried on by the wealthy merchants of Makkah and Ṭā'if. The weak were living like sheep under the strong who behaved like wolves.

The essence of the Message of God had become lost. The Christians had forgotten the teachings of Christ, the Jews disobeyed the Commandments of God, and the pagans returned to their worship of wooden and stone idols. Thus there arose an urgent need for another Messenger of God who would lead humanity back towards the worship of the One God. In the past, the Messages and the Messengers were of a localised nature pertaining to a particular group of people. A very important change that took place in the history of civilisation was that the world population had come closer together and there was now no need for the division of mankind, into different groups, for the call towards One God. Sufficient advancement had taken place that the Message could be delivered to all. Thus a Prophet was to be assigned by Allah on the basis of the universality of the Message to mankind. The pagans were not aware, but knowledgeable Christians and Jews were awaiting a Prophet to lead mankind towards the Right Path as directed by Allah.

> *I will raise them up a Prophet from among their brethren, like unto thee, and will put My words in his mouth; and he shall speak unto them all that I shall command him.*
> (Deuteronomy, 18: 18)

> *Nevertheless I tell you the truth, it is expedient for you that I go away, for if I go not away, the comforter will not come unto you; but if I depart, I will send him unto you. And when he is come, he will reprove the world of sin, and of righteousness, and of judgement.*
> (John, 17: 8)

In spite of the chaotic state of the world at that time, Allah selected His Messenger at the best time, at the best place, and sent him to the best people for a revolution to occur. The time was most appropriate as the world civilisation was entering a new phase of inter-mixing, leaving behind the old trend of clan-dominated isolation. This period was a boundary line, between the old epoch of dogmatic outlook and a new one with its rational approach. The time was also suitable in the sense that humanity was frustrated and was ready and waiting for a saviour.

If we consider the selection of the most appropriate place for delivery of the Message, Arabia was best placed. Though not a rich country, it occupied a strategic position at the centre of the trade routes. All caravans, from the East, West or North, passed through Arabia. In trade the Arabs acted as middle-men. The caravans travelling between Amman and Yemen, Sanaa and Makkah, Jeddah and Yanbu', Madinah and Dumat al-Jandal had to obtain right of passage from the Quraysh. Thus Arabia was the centre-point for India, China, Iran, Iraq, Egypt, Rome and Abyssinia.

Being an infertile region, Arabia had not been plundered and was thus left independent without control by a foreign power. The whole country was socio-politically in a liquid state.

Arabia was also centrally placed in relation to the activities of earlier Prophets. In the North was the city of Ur, the region of Ibrāhīm (*as*) and a short distant from Ur, further North, was the region of Nūḥ (*as*). Other Prophets had also worked around this area. Hence it was the best place to initiate missionary work for this area as past incidents could easily be cited.

The human resources of Arabia were also much better compared to those of Rome and Persia. The Arabs had many weaknesses, but they were still dominated by virtue because of bedouin simplicity. They were hard workers, brave and hospitable. Their memory was also strong. They were far from being hypocritical. Though it was hard for them to accept anything, once they did, they adhered to and acted upon it. They were not opportunists or double-minded, sitting on the fence. The human material that was the first recipient of the Qur'ān was the best available at that time. Their bedouin character was an additional factor to make them strive hard for material progress and development.

Revelation of the Qur'ān from the landscape of Arabia in the larger vista of history may be likened to the radiant light emanating from a bright lamp in the middle of a world that had sunk into deep and impenetrable darkness.

CHAPTER FIVE

Prophethood

5.1 Muḥammad (peace be upon him)

The recipient of the Word of God, the future Prophet, was born in Arabia on 22 April 570 CE. His birth was normal by human standards, and he was named Muḥammad (the praised one). His father died a few months before his birth. His grandfather, 'Abd al-Muṭṭalib, a prominent figure in Makkah took charge of him when he was six years old when his mother also died. His uncle, Abū Ṭālib, became Muḥammad's guardian following the death of 'Abd al-Muṭṭalib when Muḥammad was eight years old.

Makkah was the traditional centre of Arabia in both religion (paganism) and trade, being the crossroads of commercial trade between East and West, North and South. 'Abū Ṭālib's clan, the Banū Hāshim, the most influential in Arabia, was part of the great Quraysh tribe that formed an important element in the oligarchy that ruled Makkah and its surrounding tribes.

As Muḥammad entered his youth, like any other young Qurayshī, he shared in the duties and rights of his society but with a revulsion to the worship of idols. He kept himself away from all quarrels, quibbles, foul utterances, abuses and provocations. Being mostly interested in peace negotiations, he was an active member of the youth league *Ḥilf al-Fuḍūl* which was formed to protect the defenceless and guarantee the safety of strangers in Makkah. Once a stranger from the

Yemen sold goods in Makkah to an influential member of a powerful local clan who subsequently neither paid the price nor returned the goods. The aggrieved seller stood up near the Ka'bah and asked for help as a stranger in the city. A group of young Qurayshites rallied to his assistance and secured the return of his goods. Pursuant to this incident a meeting, also attended by Muḥammad (peace be upon him), was held in the house of 'Abdullāh. The attendees formed the league and pledged, henceforth, to combat oppressive acts and uphold justice. Muḥammad (peace be upon him) was then 22 years old. Even during his mission as a Prophet, he continued to express both his high regard for the league and his willingness to abide by its provisions.

At the time that the Ka'bah was being rebuilt, there arose an argument regarding the placing of the 'Black Stone'. Members of different tribes were arguing that it was their right to place the stone. Apparently, this arguing would have developed into a tribal war if something had not been done quickly to settle it. To avoid this, there was a proposal that the next person to come by would be asked to resolve the issue. When Muḥammad appeared, everyone knew that the situation would now be settled satisfactorily. He spread a cloak on the ground, put the stone on it, and then requested the representatives of the different tribes to hold the cloak and carry it towards the wall of the Ka'bah. He himself then placed the stone in its proper position. Muḥammad, like the rest of the young men in Abū Ṭālib's family, had to work and help preserve the dignity of a generation of proud and powerful Banū Hāshim.

During Muḥammad's youth, the general impression about him was that he was the most well-mannered among his people, solicitous of his neighbours, tolerant and forbearing, truthful and trustworthy. People would leave their valuables in his custody as they knew he would never betray them. While participating in business, his relations with his people made him a custodian, an unfailing trustee with the title *al-amīn* (trustworthy).

Muḥammad was a successful businessman and possessed the potential for greatness. His qualities greatly impressed Khadījah, a 40-year-old business woman who had been widowed. She married Muḥammad when he was 25 years of age. Khadījah was one of the leading merchants of Makkah and upon the union taking place, a vast field of business in Arabia and outside was thrown open to Muḥammad and he then had the opportunity to pursue a materially prosperous life.

However, worldly affluence held no attraction for him and he deliberately chose a contrary lifestyle. After marriage, relieved of his financial burden, he plunged into a quest for Truth and reality. His restless soul did not find satisfaction in material wealth; instead he pondered over the mysteries of creation, of life and death, of good and evil, and tried to seek order and light amidst chaos and gloom.

He sought answers from within himself: Where do I come from? To what end am I destined? Why do my people worship these self-made idols? Who is the Creator and what is the purpose of life? He used to retire to the solitude of a cave in Mount Ḥirā' and stay there till his meagre supply of food and water was exhausted. He would then return to his house to replenish the supplies and go back again to the solitude of nature for Prayer and meditation; to find answers to the questions surging in his mind.

The Qur'ān describes this phase of pre-prophethood in the following words:

> *Did He not find you an orphan, and gave you shelter? And found you lost on your way, and guided you? And found you in want, and gave you sufficiency?*
>
> (Aḍ-Ḍuḥā, 93: 6–8)

His quest had reached a point when life had become an unbearable burden. Allah reminds the Prophet (peace be upon him) about this past situation:

> *Have We not opened up your heart, and lifted from you the burden that had weighed so heavily on your back?*
> (Al-Inshirāḥ, 94: 1–3)

5.2 Prophethood

Muḥammad (peace be upon him) settled into a peaceful family life, but he still pondered over many unanswered questions. He dwelt on the phenomena of human existence, the basic questions about God, life after death, and the relationship between man and God. He would think about this and, as we have stated, found peace by going to a cave in the mountains, known now as 'Cave Ḥirā', and it was here that the very first Revelation came.

> 'Read!' said the voice.
>
> 'I am not of those who read.'
>
> 'Read!'
>
> 'I am not of those who read.'
>
> 'Read!'
>
> 'I am not of those who read.'
>
> 'Read!'
>
> 'What shall I read?'
>
> *Read in the name of your Lord Who created, created man from a clot! Read for your Lord is most generous, (it is He) Who teaches by means of the pen, teaches man what he does not know.*
>
> (Al-'Alaq, 96: 1–5)

Upon hearing these words, Muḥammad (peace be upon him) rushed home to his wife Khadījah and sat shivering, unable to believe what he had heard. His wife covered him with a blanket and consoled him. It seems that after those verses there was an interruption (*fatrah*) the duration of which cannot exactly be ascertained, being from about six months to perhaps two years. During this period, Muḥammad (peace be upon him) was uncertain as to what was expected of him. He became worried as time went by without any further signs.

Muḥammad (peace be upon him) then started to receive answers to his questions. The greatest event of history that was destined to transform his land, his people and the whole of humanity occurred when he heard a voice commanding him:

> *'You are the Messenger of Allah, and I am Gabriel.'*
> *O you (in your solitude) enfolded! Arise and warn! (Give up now your solitude, and stand up before all the world as a preacher and warner). And your Sustainer's greatness glorify! And your inner self purify! And all defilement shun! And do not through giving seek yourself to gain, but unto your Sustainer turn in patience.*
>
> (Al-Muddaththir, 74: 1–7)

This was the beginning of the relationship between the Message and the Messenger. It is this Message which is introduced and discussed in this book – the words that conquered the hearts of the multitudes and continue to do so with soaring vitality now more than fourteen centuries later.

Muḥammad's unique position in religious history is due to the fact that he inspired all he did without being a saint or an angel, without having any attributes which were not strictly human. People said he was mad. But then certain verses from *Sūrah al-Qalam* were revealed to him:

> *Nūn, by the pen and by the (Record) which (men) write – You are not, by the grace of your Lord, mad or possessed.*
>
> (Al-Qalam, 68: 1–2)

No, he was not mad. He emerged as the most influential person in history. Prophet Muḥammad (peace be upon him) and the Qur'ān were complementary to each other. The Qur'ān inspired the Prophet and the Prophet personified the Qur'ān. Thus, through the Qur'ān and his illuminating personality, the Prophet was able to unite a people that were scattered, and transform them into a strong community by establishing a new order based on Divine Guidance.

What a tremendous change was brought by the Qur'ān and Prophet Muḥammad (peace be upon him) in the Arabs, the proudest people at that time on earth. This is the reason why Goethe, the greatest of German poets, speaking about the Holy Qur'ān, declared that, 'This book will go on exercising through all ages a most potent influence.' This is also the reason why George Bernard Shaw said, 'If any religion has a chance of ruling over England, nay, Europe, within the next 100 years, it is Islam.'

5.3 The Man-Prophet

Muḥammad (peace be upon him) commenced his life's journey as an orphan and ended it as the head of a state. While enjoying total authority, especially after the bloodless conquest of Makkah, he led the same way of life, using the same bedding mat woven out of palm leaves, wearing the same patched clothes and mending his own shoes.

> *And We have not sent you but as a mercy to all the worlds.*
>
> (Al-Anbiyā', 21: 107)

His morals and manners were but a reflection of the teachings of the Qur'ān. Uprightness was his most outstanding trait. Simplicity characterised him. Generosity was his second nature and humility his very essence.

Instead of cursing his persecutors, he would raise his hands and say, 'O Allah! Forgive them, for they know not.' 'O Lord! Guide my people right.' In the matter of justice he did not make any distinction between Muslim and non-Muslim. His equity, integrity and impartiality were well known. Between employee and employer the Prophet (peace be upon him) was committed to justice and fair dealing.

He was indeed a model, a pattern, an example in all aspects of life, with his career covering almost all aspects of life. To man, the model must be a man and a man-Prophet he was, so that he could serve as a model for all men and for all times to come.

The mission of the Prophet was to make people God-conscious. Muḥammad (peace be upon him) was the herald of a great revolution for all mankind to remove conflicts and stagnation and to raise mankind to the higher plane of peace and progress. Muḥammad (peace be upon him) was a revolutionary Prophet, ushering in a revolution of peace not only to end the feuds of families, tribes and nations but of all mankind.

Revolutionary Prophet though he was, he did not put himself on a high pedestal, or in an ivory tower beyond the reach of man. He was no mystical figure. He was no demi-god. This Messenger of Allah repeatedly claimed to be but a man, in his own words, 'like unto others'. This human Prophet came for the good of mankind, for persons of all climes, all countries. He was a man, among mankind, a leader and benefactor of persons, a model and an example for all and for ever. May his name be ever praised!

The only way to praise him is to follow in his footsteps in day-to-day living, to so chisel and so shape oneself to become 'like unto him'. His name be ever praised!

5.4 The Finality of Prophethood

Allah in His mercy and wisdom selected the Prophet (peace be upon him) amongst the caretakers of the Ka'bah, the House of God. The purpose of Revelation remained the same, to guide mankind towards the fundamentals of the Divine life-style – the Oneness of God, the accountability of man's actions in the world, and Life-after-Death for the reward and punishment of actions in this world. In addition, this time, was the finality of prophethood. Allah planned that the first era of subjugation to nature and dependence upon supernatural occurrences be finished, and the second, or final era of enlightenment, and the conquest of nature by mankind, start with the advent of this last Prophet. This age of enlightenment demanded that human beings themselves attain the level of comprehension and understanding to carry on the duty of the propagation of the Divine Message. In other words, the followers of the last universal Prophet (peace be upon him) were asked to perform the task of the Prophet and accept responsibility for the propagation of Islam.

Hence, as in other Revealed Books, the Qur'ān embodies one Divine Message, known as *Islām* (i.e. submission to Allah). Adam (*as*) the first man was Muslim and Muḥammad (peace be upon him) the last Prophet was Muslim and the Prophets and Messengers in between were also Muslims, as were all the true followers of the Prophets. The true followers of Moses, Christ and Muḥammad all were Muslims.

CHAPTER SIX

The Message and the Messenger

6.1 The Absoluteness of Ethics

In spite of all wisdom and intellect human beings are finite in space and time, limited to their environment and surroundings. Like air, sunshine and natural resources man needs a framework and guidance for his lifestyle. Naturally, the only Being that can provide the basis of living on this planet is the Creator, the Controller and Sustainer Himself. The relativeness of human involvement should be replaced with the absolute ethics provided by Allah. These absolute ethics, Divine in origin, should be regarded as such, and as being in conformity with human nature. Thus Divine Guidance may be provided in different languages and different methods, but there should not be any basic departure from its ethics. Hence, whatever differences may appear in religion and whatever hatred may be developed among the followers of different religions, their ethics and standards of morality should be the same. The source of all ethics is nothing else but Allah (God). Any kind of morality found and propounded by non-religious persons or agnostics is also due to their indirect contact with revealed knowledge through ancestors or the society in which they live.

The Qur'ān and other Revealed Scriptures are the outcome of the same Divine Messages. Differences in modes of expression or changes in the texts are due to human intervention. The Qur'ān, of all Revelations, is the only one preserved in its original form, has been for 1400 years, and will remain preserved for eternity. Thus the authenticity and correctness of all Divine Messages may be verified on the basis of the approach and Message of the Qur'ān.

6.2 Muḥammad (peace be upon him) and the Qur'ān

The absoluteness of ethics and the perfect model of the followers of these ethics should be both universal and lasting. The guidance from Allah, in principle, is based on one ethic that was manifested in different versions as human beings continued their journey in the realm of civilisation. The mental and physical development of civilisation arrived at a stage of enlightenment that did not require further modifications of guidance from Allah. The Message of the Qur'ān and the model of the Messenger Muḥammad (peace be upon him) are comprehensive enough, and humanity is developed enough to live by the two, taking them as eternal and lasting.

Prophets are unique persons who carry on the mission of changing human beings from within. Prophets influence not only individuals, but have a great impact on the social order of their times. The Messengers and the Message are complementary to each other to the extent that no lifestyle can be comprehended or practised without the assimilation of the two – the Words of God and the demonstration of the Prophets to act upon these words. The Message, when isolated from the Messenger, is like a ship without a captain by which the unskilled passengers cannot reach their destination whoever they may be. The Messenger, not related with the Message, can be misconstrued as God Himself. Hinduism is an example of the first, and Christianity the second. Prophet Muḥammad (peace be upon him) overhauled the whole of society by changing the approach and outlook of human beings. He proved himself to be the saviour of mankind. He ushered in a new era of enlightenment and brought about a conceptual renaissance in developing first the Islamic civilisation and then carrying on its impact to this day in the making of human civilisation.

To comprehend the Message and appreciate the Qur'ān, one has to study the life of the Prophet (*Sunnah*) and then apply the Qur'ān and the *Sunnah* in daily living to be a true follower of Islam. This background makes it clear that the Qur'ān basically changes the psyche, the outlook of human beings to such an extent that people motivated and influenced by the Qur'ān take on the leadership of mankind. The Qur'ān is not a book of philosophy, theology or science. It changes one's viewpoint in such a way that the personality of its recipient is transformed. The reader starts seeing everything from a different point of view; a new criterion is developed to evaluate events, and thus insight is developed for decision-making. Hence if the Qur'ān is understood and followed in day-to-day living, a society emerges that inculcates peace, and helps make this world a place with equal opportunities.

The instructions of God – the Qur'ān, and the practise of these instructions by the Prophet Muḥammad (peace be upon him) – documented in the *Sunnah*, produced a group of people that revolutionised the world. The personality of the Arabs, the direct recipients of the Qur'ān and the *Sunnah* was dramatically changed. The most uncivilised became fully civilised, the illiterate became literate, the dogmatic became rational, and then through these Arabs and other followers of Islam, a new and forceful Islamic civilisation flourished for 300 years and its impact is still apparent in Western civilisation. The question arises as to why the impact of the Qur'ān and the *Sunnah* has not enabled Muslims to dominate this world. The answer is, quite obviously, that the present Muslims have affinity neither with the Qur'ān nor with the Prophet Muḥammad (peace be upon him). The Qur'ān and the *Sunnah* can mould the life of any person who takes a keen interest in understanding and is prepared to act upon it whether he or she is a born Muslim or not.

6.3 Following the Ordinance of the Prophet (peace be upon him)

> *But nay, by the Sustainer; They do not (really) believe unless they make you (O Prophet) a judge of all on which they disagree among themselves, and then find in their hearts no bar to the acceptance of your decision and give themselves up (to it) in utter self surrender.*
>
> (An-Nisā', 4: 65)

This verse lays down, in an unequivocal manner, the obligation of every Muslim to submit to the ordinances which the Prophet (peace be upon him), under Divine inspiration, promulgated with a view to exemplifying the Message of the Qur'ān and enabling the Believers to apply it to actual situations. These ordinances constitute what is described as the authenticated *sunnah* (way) of the Prophet Muḥammad (peace be upon him) and have full legal force side by side with the Qur'ān.

The following verse clarifies the position of the Prophet (peace be upon him):

> *We have sent you forth as a Messenger to mankind. Allah is (your) all sufficient witness. He who obeys the Messenger obeys Allah Himself. For those who pay no heed to you, know then that We have not sent you to watch over them.*
>
> (An-Nisā', 4: 79–80)

6.4 Manifestation of the Word of Allah

Subsequently there came other verses, time after time, year after year, in accordance with certain incidents and circumstances. The period of Revelation lasted 22 years and 5 months, from 610 to 632 CE. A total of 4,825 verses were revealed in Makkah during the first 13 years and 1,314 verses in the Madinan period. From the very first Revelation, all subsequent Revelations of the Word of Allah were written down, whether on parchment, paper, the bones of animals, the skins of animals or the bark of trees, etc. It was recorded by 40 Companions of the Prophet (peace be upon him), who were known as *Kuttāb al-Waḥy* or Writers of Revelation. Whenever a Revelation was received the Prophet (peace be upon him) ordered these writers to memorise it and keep a written document in the order it was revealed at a certain place. The Prophet (peace be upon him) checked this. The most prominent writers among the Companions were Abū Bakr al-Ṣiddīq, 'Uthmān, 'Alī, Zayd ibn Thābit and 'Abdullāh ibn Mas'ūd. It was the habit of the Prophet (peace be upon him) to recite the whole Qur'ān and the Angel Gabriel used to listen to him. This was the normal practice of the Prophet (peace be upon him) during the holy month of Ramaḍān, when the Prophet (peace be upon him) used to recite the Qur'ān once. However, during the last Ramaḍān of his life he recited the Qur'ān twice.

After the Prophet's (peace be upon him) death, when Abū Bakr was the first Caliph, many Muslims were killed by their enemies. In order to survive and protect their religion and land, the Muslims became engaged in a number of wars on various fronts. In one of the battles, at Yamāmah, a large contingent of Muslims who knew the Qur'ān by heart were killed. 'Umar ibn al-Khaṭṭāb then realised that there was a grave danger that the Qur'ān might be lost and knowledge of the great Book be affected. He discussed this with the Caliph, Abū Bakr, who after some hesitation agreed to the compilation of the Qur'ān, so that it could be protected from any loss. Under the third Caliph, ‘Uthmān (*ra*), this manuscript was reproduced as the *Muṣḥaf* (the Book), copies of which were sent to different countries. The present Qur’ān is a copy of the *Muṣḥaf* at the time of ‘Uthmān (*ra*).

CHAPTER SEVEN

Themes of the Qur'ān

7.1 Divine Lifestyle

Islam is a religion in the sense that its tenets are based on Divine Guidance but Islam is not a religion as religion is perceived today. Since its foundation is based on logic and reasoning and not on dogma or blind faith, the fact of not compartmentalising the secular and religious spheres into separate enclosures indicates that Islam is more a God-directed whole system of life and not a religion dealing with compartments, or sections of life. Hence on the one side, when dealing with the principles of living – social, political or economic – Islam may be compared with non-religious ideologies like capitalism, communism, socialism, etc. and when dealing with the moral and spiritual development of individuals and societies, it can be compared with other religions such as Hinduism, Buddhism, Judaism and Christianity.

The three basic tenets of Islam – The Oneness of God, Life-after-Death and the Guidance of God (Revelation) – are to be accepted with full reasoning and rationality. Second, Islam deals with all aspects of human life. Islam is not confined to the spiritual development of human beings. It is vehemently against the idea of segregating the secular and religious, material and spiritual, this worldly and the Other World. Thus Islam proposes the unity not only of ideas but also of actions.

According to Islam, the One Almighty God, Allah, created and appointed mankind as His vicegerent on earth with autonomy. Life in this world is a period of test, and reward or punishment is in the life Hereafter. Allah arranged the receiving of His guidance throughout the ages through His chosen persons known as Prophets. The first vicegerent and Prophet was Adam (*as*) and the whole of mankind is his progeny. All the Prophets or Messengers had one religion, Islam, and one mission of inviting people and mobilising those who accept the invitation.

The fundamental theme of the Qur'ān is that Allah always offers guidance to man through the Revelations which He bestows upon His Prophets. In this way the Qur'ān leads towards principles that are central to ethical rectitude and beneficial to man's individual and social life. It is guidance for the life-span of the whole community

> *Verily, this Qur'ān shows the way to all that is most upright and gives the believers who do good deeds the glad tidings that theirs will be a great reward, and (it announces, also), that We have readied suffering for them who do not believe in the life to come.*
>
> (Al-Isrā', 17: 9–10)

7.2 Foundational Message

Islam is a combination of the Divine Revelation – the Qur'ān – and its recipient, the Prophet Muḥammad (peace be upon him) . These two are inseparable and represent the Words of God and the model of these words in action. The Qur'ān and Muḥammad (peace be upon him) have the capacity to mould multi-cultural, multi-ethnic groups of people of different territories, races, languages and political systems into one *Ummah* (community).

The Qur'ān is an eternal Message and at its fountainhead God is eternal, for ever and ever. It is a Message for all times and for all climes and countries. It is a Message not only for Muslims but for all mankind. The Qur'ān is not the first Message of God but is actually the final dissemination. Its mission was not to introduce a new Message but to endorse with fresh vigour the Message delivered earlier to Abraham, David, Moses, Jesus and other Prophets.

The Qur'ān revolves around the concept of *Tawḥīd* (Unity of God). Belief in *Tawḥīd* binds and unites all the other parts of the Qur'ān. The God of the Qur'ān is not a tribal, racial, national nor regional type of god.

As a corollary, to believe in the Unity of God, the Qur'ān follows belief in the Oneness of humanity. In this way, then, the Qur'ān presented a revolutionary outlook. It broke all the barriers of time and place, race and colour and made a unique contribution to the growth of human civilisation by propounding the theory of one humanity – the children of Adam, the family of man.

> *Verily, this community of yours is a single community (nation).*
>
> (Al-Anbiyā', 21: 92)

> *O ye men! We have created you of a male and a female, and made you tribes and families that you may know each other.*
>
> (Al-Ḥujurāt, 49: 13)

Thus nations and races are basically for the purpose of easy reference, for identification only and not for dividing humanity into confrontational chauvinistic groupings. In the Qur'ān, mankind is the central theme. The restoration of the rightful place to each individual is one of the major teachings of the Qur'ān. The Qur'ān attempts to implement its theme, 'One God, One Humanity', by instructing mankind to raise the level of its morality.

The Qur'ān uses a new word for religion, namely *dīn*. Religion is not seen as a set of dogmas and doctrines nor rituals and ceremonies. In Qur'ānic usage *dīn* is a code of conduct, a way of life, an ideology and a dynamic movement. The Qur'ān calls this *dīn* Islam.

The Qur'ān is the first Book of religion in the history of mankind to spell out the dynamic concept of an undivided humanity – the family of man, the children of Adam.

> *O ye men! We have created you of a male and a female.*
> (Al-Ḥujurāt, 49: 13)

The Qur'ān urges the whole of mankind, all the people of the world, to raise themselves above parochial, tribal, racial and national limitations. The Qur'ān propounds universality.

According to the Qur'ān, good deeds and righteous living are manifested by love and mercy, justice and kindness, respect for covenants, purity and chastity. These are indeed the yardsticks to measure right and wrong, good and evil.

> *It is not virtue to turn your faces to the East or the West. But the real virtue lies in believing in Allah. . .*
> (Al-Baqarah, 2: 177)

7.3 Self-Surrender to Allah

> *The only true faith in Allah's sight is Islam (self-surrender unto Allah). Those who were vouchsafed revelation aforetime took, out of mutual jealousy, divergent views (on this point) only after knowledge (thereof) had come unto them. He that denies Allah's revelations should know that He is swift in reckoning.*
>
> *If they argue with you, say: 'I have surrendered myself to Allah and so have those that follow me.'*
>
> *To those who have received the kitāb (divine writ) and to the Ummiyīn (people having no revealed Scripture of their own), say: 'Will you surrender yourself to Allah.' If they become Muslims (surrender themselves to Allah),*

they are on the right path. If they turn away, your duty is no more than to deliver the message: Allah is watching over all His servants.

(Āl 'Imrān, 3: 19–20)

The following verses carry a wider import and relate to all communities which base their views on a Revealed Scripture, extant in a partially corrupted form, some parts of which are entirely lost. All these communities at first subscribed to the doctrine of Allah's Oneness and held that Islam (man's self-surrender to Allah) is the essence of all true religion. Their subsequent divergence was the outcome of sectarian pride and mutual exclusiveness:

And (remember) when Allah made His covenant with the Prophets, (He said): 'Here are the revelations and the wisdom which I have given you. A Messenger will come forth to confirm them. Believe in him and help him.

Do you acknowledge and accept My bond on this condition?'

They replied: 'We do acknowledge it.'

Then bear witness', He said, 'and I will bear witness with you. He who after this rebels is a transgressor.'

Do they seek, perchance, a faith other than in Allah, although it is unto Him that whatever is in the heavens and on earth surrenders itself, willingly or by compulsion, since unto Him all must return? Say: 'We believe in Allah and what is revealed to us, in that which was revealed to Ibrāhīm (as) and Ismā'īl (as) to Isḥāq (as) and Ya'qūb (as) and their descendants; and in that which their Lord gave Mūsā (as) and 'Īsā (as) and (other) Prophets. We make no distinction between any of them. To Him we have surrendered ourselves.

He who chooses a religion other than Islam (self-

> *surrender unto Allah), it will not be accepted from him, and in the world to come he will be among the losers.*
> (Āl 'Imrān, 3 : 81–5)

7.4 The Qur'ān and Consciousness of Allah

The essential aspect of the Qur'ānic teaching is to awaken in the human being the higher consciousness of his manifest relationship with God. According to the Qur'ān, the affirmation of spirit does not come by the renunciation of the external forces but by proper adjustment of man's relation to these forces in view of the light of the world received from within. Thus the spiritual animates and sustains the material. The Qur'ān demands the affirmation of the spiritual self in man with a recognition of his contact with the world of matter, and it points the way to master it, with a view to discovering a basis for a realistic regulation of life.

The Qur'ān directs two ways of establishing connection with the reality that confronts human beings: one is the direct association with reality as it reveals itself within a person, that is, the inner experience; the other is the indirect reflective observation and utilisation of natural phenomena as they reveal themselves to perception. The Qur'ān regards both *Anfus* (self) and *Āfāq* (world) as sources of knowledge. Allah reveals these signs in inner, as well as outer, experience and it is the duty of human beings to judge the knowledge-yielding capacity of all aspects of experience. Thus there are three main sources of human knowledge referred to in the Qur'ān, namely inner perception, environment (Signs of Allah) and History (the Days of Allah).

Inner Perception

> *Such is He Who knows all that is beyond the reach of a created being's perception, as well as all that can be witnessed by a creature's senses or mind: the Almighty, the Dispenser of Grace, Who makes excellent everything*

that He creates. And He begins the creation of man out of clay; then He causes him to be begotten out of the essence of a humble fluid; and then He forms him in accordance with what he is meant to be, and breathes into him of His spirit: and (these O people) He endows you with hearing, sight and insights: (yet) how seldom are you grateful.

(As-Sajdah, 32: 6–9)

The Qur'ān recognises that an empirical attitude is an indispensable stage in the spiritual life of humanity and thus it gives equal importance to all the facets of human experience as yielding knowledge of the Ultimate Reality which reveals its symbols both within and without. According to the Qur'ān, to secure a complete vision of Reality, sensory perception must be supplemented by the perception of *Fu'ād* or the heart as revealed in the above verse. The heart provides inner intuition or inner experience that brings us into contact with aspects of Reality other than those open to the senses. Mystically information is disseminated to the mind. It is a mode of dealing with Reality in which sensation, in the physiological sense of the word, does not play any part.

The region of inner experience, for the purpose of knowledge, is as real as any other region of human experience and cannot be traced back to sensory perception. The immediacy of inner experience resembles our normal experience and belongs to the same category. Unfortunately, living in the present world of naked materialism, we have assumed, without criticism, that knowledge of the external world through sensory perception is knowledge. Allah reveals in the Qur'ān:

When My servants question you about Me, tell them that I am near. I answer the Prayer of the suppliant when he calls to Me, that he may be rightly guided.

(Al-Baqarah, 2: 186)

Environment

The Qur'ān sees the Signs of Allah in the sun, the moon, the lengthening of shadows, the alternation of night and day, the variety of human colour and language – in fact the whole environment as revealed to the sensory perception of a human being. A Muslim's duty is to reflect on these signs and not to pass them by 'as if he is deaf and blind', for the one 'who does not see these signs in his life will remain blind to the realities of the life to come'.

The immediate purpose of the Qur'ān in this reflective observation of the environment is to awaken in man the consciousness that his surroundings are to be regarded as a tool.

History

History, or in the words of the Qur'ān 'the days of Allah', is the third source of human knowledge. The Qur'ān constantly cites historical instances and urges its readers to reflect upon the past and the present experiences of mankind, and realise that they are judged and have to suffer for their misdeeds.

> *We formerly sent Moses with Our Signs (saying): 'Lead your people out of the darkness into the light, and remind them of the days of Allah.' Surely in this are Signs for every steadfast, grateful person.*
>
> (Ibrāhīm, 14: 5)

> *Already, before your time, have precedents been made to roam the world and see what was the fate of those who rejected the Signs of Allah.*
>
> (Āl 'Imrān, 3: 137)

CHAPTER EIGHT

The Book of Knowledge

8.1 A Unique Book

The Qur'ān is the last guidance for mankind revealed by Allah to Muḥammad (peace be upon him). It is not a man-written book on the subject of the religion of Islam but rather the compilation of Divine Revelations spread over 23 years.

The unique characteristic of the Qur'ān, being the Word of God revealed and compiled 1400 years ago, makes it distinct and different from conventional books. Just as Islam is not a mere conventional religion, the Qur'ān too is not a conventional book.

Being a collection of timely Divine directions according to circumstances, it is quite different from what can be considered a normal book. Generally a book has an introduction, chapters, a central theme and then sub-themes relating to that chapter. The chapters are also related to each other, at least in the sense of describing different aspects of the same subject, for which the book is geared. The Qur'ān does not conform to this conventional notion of a book. The title, 'Al-Qur'ān' and those of most of its chapters (*sūrahs*) do not depict the exact theme of the Book or those of the chapters.

The Qur'ān has to be comprehended not just on its explicit setting but on its implicit nature and its style based on the linguistic and temporal atmosphere. Let us take the titles of the chapters (*sūrahs*). For example, the title of the second *Sūrah*, *Al-Baqarah*, is translated in English as 'The Cow'. A person would then expect that this chapter will deal with the main theme of the Cow. At first glance, the connection seems confusing. However, when examined closely, the relationship between the title and the theme becomes clearer. *Sūrah al-Baqarah* deals with the mischief and the follies committed by the Banī Isrā'īl, that is, the children of Ya'qūb (Jacob) through Isḥāq (Isaac), and the most conspicuous event was their disobedience to the commandment of God, in slaughtering a cow, and how they wrongly accused their Messenger.

Every language has its own pattern of comprehension and idiom. In the Arabic language and especially at the time of the Qur'ān's compilation, the titles of the chapters (*sūrahs*) were not fixed on the basis of the main theme but were selected on the basis of a key word of the corresponding chapter.

The Qur'ān is a collection of piecemeal Revelations of the Word of Allah made to Prophet Muḥammad (peace be upon him) on different occasions over 23 years. The Prophet (peace be upon him) was ordained to call humanity towards the Right Path and the Revelations were made in order to help him in carrying out this duty of initiating and establishing an Islamic order. Once the movement became successful and a new community was formed, there arose the need for guidance. The revealed verses were thus compiled in a different sequence to that of their actual Revelation.

The Revelation is designed to offer Islam the Message of God and to convince humanity to embrace Islam. Once a community of the followers of Islam (*Ummah*) was formed, the need arose for compilation of the same Revelation in an order that could educate and allow the Believers to follow Islam in the true sense.

The revelational sequence is movement-oriented while the compilation sequence is community-oriented and universal. If one has to invite non-Muslims and explain to them the basic tenets of Islam by producing relevant evidence, it is advisable to use the sequential order. The Muslim community has to use the Qur'ān as their guide.

To understand the nature of the Qur'ān, we have to appreciate the difference between the Word of God and words written by human beings. The Word of God is implicit in the sense that its meaning changes with the level of comprehension by human beings and is eternal in the sense that it is valid for all times. The man-written words are explicit, having clear meaning and are temporal, being valid for a particular time. The universal nature of the Qur'ān has made the coherence of the compilatory order implicit. Thus the Qur'ān, the original source of solving the differences, or the criterion for decision-making, implies different interpretations in different times to enable an updating in comprehension in accordance with the intellectual level of mankind.

8.2 The Qur'ān and Science

The uniqueness of the revealed knowledge bestowed upon mankind by Allah (*swt*) through the Qur'ān is to instruct humanity in a scientific way. With the advent of the Qur'ān, humanity entered the scientific age. The Qur'ān, in fact, is the first and last Divine Revelation which teaches man to reflect on the fundamentals of nature, the creation of the heavens and the earth, the change of seasons, rotation of day and night, the sea, the clouds, the winds, the sun, the moon, the stars and the laws they obey.

The Qur'ān bids mankind to ponder over the mysteries of birth and death, and the growth and decay of individuals and nations. The Qur'ān asks man to contemplate the sunset, the dawn, hills, streams, ravines, vineyards, the canopy of the starry heaven, the ships sailing on the sea.

In the creation of the heavens and the earth; in the alternation of night and day; in the ships that sail the ocean with what is beneficial to man; in the water which Allah sends down from the sky and with which He revives the earth after its death, dispersing over it all manner of beasts; in the movements of the winds, and in the clouds that are driven between earth and sky; surely in these there are Signs for people who understand.

(Al-Baqarah, 2: 164)

In the creation of the heavens and the earth, and in the alternation of night and day, there are Signs for men of understanding.

(Āl 'Imrān, 3: 190)

It was Allah Who raised the heavens without visible pillars. He then ascended His throne and fixed the sun and the moon into His service, each pursuing an appointed course. He ordains all things. He makes plain His revelations so that you may firmly believe in meeting your Lord.

(Ar-Ra'd 13: 2)

Allah brought you out of your mother's womb devoid of all knowledge, and gave you ears and eyes and hearts, so that you may give thanks.

Do they not see the birds that wing their flight in heaven's vault? None sustains them but Allah. Surely in this there are Signs for true believers.

(An-Naḥl, 16: 78–9)

It was He Who created you from dust, then from a life-germ, and then a clot of blood. He then brings you forth as a child, then (lets you) reach manhood, and then grow into old age – though some of you die young – so that you may reach an appointed term, and understand.

(Ghāfir, 40: 67)

It is Allah Who made the heavens and the earth, and sends down water from the sky with which He brings forth fruits for your sustenance. He drives the ships which, by His leave, sail the ocean in your service. He has created rivers for your benefit, and the sun and the moon, which steadfastly pursue their courses. And He has subdued to you the night and the day.

(Ibrāhīm, 14: 32–3)

He set firm mountains upon the earth lest it should move away with you; and rivers, and landmarks, so that you may be rightly guided. By the stars, too, are men directed.

(An-Naḥl, 16: 15–16)

Because of the inspiration from and thorough understanding of the Qur'ān, Muslim scientists emerged as the leaders of the renaissance in the field of Natural Sciences. Let us then take a brief look at some of these contributions to mankind's progress.

Jurisprudence

1. Recognition of the personal liberty and rights of women and children.
2. Establishment of equality of all in the eyes of the law.
3. A new branch of Juristic Science known as Applied Science of Testimony (using precedence in courts of law).

History and Sociology

Ibn Baṭṭūṭah (d.1377 CE); Aṭ-Ṭabarī (d.923 CE); Al-Mas'ūdī (d.956 CE).

Al-Mas'ūdī (d.956 CE)	Monumental work on Universal History up to 947 CE.

Ibn Ḥayyān (d.1076 CE)	History of Spain.
Abu'l Faraj al-Asfahānī) (d.976 CE)	Book of songs (and Arab Poetry) (21 volumes).
Al-Bīrūnī (d.1048 CE)	Principles of historical criticism.
Al-Khaṭīb al-Baghdādī (d.1376 CE)	60 works on different subjects.
Ibn 'Asākir (d.1177 CE)	Biographies of distinguished men of Damascus.
Ibn Khaldūn (d.1406 CE)	Political Theory, History of Philosophy and Sociology, Theory of Historical Development and Founder of the Science of Sociology.

Geography

Al-Khawārizmī (d.847 CE)	Map of the heavenly bodies and the world.
Al-Muqaddasī (9th century)	Geographical Encyclopaedia.
Al-Iṣṭakhrī (10th century)	Geography of the Islamic World with coloured maps for each country.
Al-Bīrūnī (d.1048 CE)	Geography of Rome and Northern Europe.
Al-Idrīsī (d.1180 CE)	Celestial Sphere; Disk-shaped map of the world.

Yāqūt ar-Rūmī (d.1229 CE)	Monumental Encyclopaedia of Geography (6 volumes).

Astronomy and Mathematics

Al-Fazārī (d.806 CE)	Translated the Sidhanta, the Indian tables, into Arabic.
Al-Khawārizmī (d.847 CE)	1. Devised his own Astronomical Tables. 2. Older Arab treatise on Arithmetic and Algebra. 3. Founder of Algebra. His book *Hisāb al-Jabr-wa'l-Muqābalah* was used until the 16th century as the principal mathematical text in European Universities.
Az-Zarqalī (d.1089 CE)	First determination of time by altitude.
Sons of Mūsā ibn Shākir	Marked for the first time the equinoxes and the movement of the solar apogee.
Abū Mash'ar (d.886 CE)	The laws of the tides based on the movement of the moon in relation to the earth.

Mathematics

'Umar al-Khayyām (d.1125 CE)	The method of solving Trigonometrical and Algebraic equations of the second degree.
Abū Bakr Muḥammad (d.1125 CE)	Solved diophantac and quadratic equations.
Al-Battānī (d.929 CE)	Discovered most of the basic notions of Trigonometrical ratio.
Abu'l Wafā' (d.998 CE)	Found the generality of the Sine Theorem in relation to the spherical triangle. Introduced the tangent, cotangent, secant and cosecant in Trigonometry.

Chemistry

Ar-Rāzī (L. Rhazes: d.925 CE)	*Kitābul Asrār* translated into Latin by Gerard and Cremon: the chief source of chemical knowledge.
Jābir ibn Ḥayyān (L. Gaber: d.776 CE)	Superseded the works of Ar-Rāzī. Devised the process of calcination and reduction. Improved the method of evaporation, sublimation, melting and crystallisation. Devised the Theory of the Constituents of Metals.

Al-Jāḥiẓ (d.868 CE)	Obtained ammonia from the offals of animals by dry distillation.

Medicine

Yaḥyā ibn Māsawayah (d.858 CE)	Textbook on Opthalmology.
Ar-Rāzī (L. Rhazes: d.923 CE)	More than 200 medical books. *Kitāb al-Manṣūrī* (10 volumes). *Al-Ḥāwī*, Encyclopaedic work.
'Alī ibn al-'Abbās (L. Haly, d.944 CE)	*Kitāb al-Mālikī* translated into Latin. Contained Materia Medica and Dietetics.
Ibn al-Haitham (d.1039 CE)	His work became the basis of Western Optics.
Ibn al-Bayṭār (d.1248 CE)	Standard Materia Medica for centuries.
Abu'l Qāsim al-Zahrāwī (d.1013 CE)	*At-Tasrīf*: A medical Encyclopaedia used in Europe for centuries as a standard work on surgery.
Ibn Rushd (L. Averroes: d.1198 CE)	A person can be infected with smallpox only once.

Ibn Sīnā (L. Avicenna: d.1037 CE)	Superseded the works of Hippocrates and Galen. Used as text-books of medicine in European Universities. *Qānūn*: chief guide to medical services in the West from 12th to 17th century CE.
Ibn Zuhr (d.1030 CE)	Discovered sensitivities in bones.
Ibn al-Khaṭīb (d.1374 CE)	Infection through contact with the afflicted and their garments, vessels and ear-rings.

Science owes much to the Qur'ān. The Qur'ān introduced a scientific method for the first time. The Greeks, because of their philosophic bent of mind, were more interested in generalities and propounding theories; they were not familiar with methods of investigation, detail and prolonged observations and experimental enquiries. The Qur'ān initiated and extended the development of a new spirit of enquiry, new methods of investigation, observations and measurements that paved the way for the scientific advancements of the following centuries.

The Qur'ān is the fountainhead of science in the sense that it was responsible for great discussions. The verses of the Qur'ān repeatedly called attention to the movement of heavenly bodies as miracles of Allah and, thus, these verses inspired Muslims to make use of the universe and its treasures instead of worshipping them.

8.3 Embryology

According to the Qur'ān, the reproduction of human beings is carried out by the implantation of the egg in the female genital organ, denoted by the word *'Alaq*.

> *Created man out of a germ-cell.*
>
> (Al-'Alaq, 96: 2)

The very first Qur'ānic Revelation alludes to man's embryonic evolution out of a 'germ-cell' – out of a fertilised ovum – thus indicating that a species of primitive and simple biological organism may attain high intellectual and spiritual development. This also shows the existence of a conscious design and a purpose underlying the creation of life.

> *Now, indeed, We created man out of the essence of clay, and then We caused him to remain as a drop of sperm in (the womb's) firm keeping:*
>
> *And then We create out of the drop of sperm a germ-cell, and then We create out of the germ-cell an embryonic lump, and then We create within the embryonic lump bones:*
>
> *And then We clothe the bones with flesh – and then We bring (all) this into being as a new creation:*
>
> *Hallowed, therefore, is Allah, the best of Creators.*
>
> *And then, behold! after all this, you are destined to die;*
>
> *And then, behold! you shall be raised from the dead on the Resurrection Day.*
>
> (Al-Mu'minūn, 23: 12–16)

The frequent Qur'ānic reference to man's being 'created out of clay' or 'out of dust' or 'out of the essence of clay', point to the fact that man's body is composed of various organic and inorganic substances existing on or in the earth. There is also a continuous transmutation of these substances, through the intake of earth-grown food into reproductive cells. Allah stresses man's humble origin and the debt of gratitude which he owes to Him.

The evolution of the embryo inside the uterus is described, in simple words, in fundamental stages of growth. The formation of the embryonic lump in the form of a 'chewed flesh' (*muḍghah*) after the germ-cell (*'alaqah*) is found to be the exact process in the formation of a child in its mother's womb. Then the bones develop inside this lump and the bones are covered with muscle. This is meant by use of the word *laḥm* (intact flesh). The process of formation is finished and then a new human being comes into existence to be separated from the mother to exist independently of her body.

What should be noted is that the Qur'ān is not a book of science which mentions the process of creation scientifically and then leaves it. The process of humans coming into being clearly points to the creative activity of Allah hence to His existence. The lack of gratitude on the part of human beings is, according to the Qur'ān, 'giving the lie to the Truth'. The purpose of providing this information is to use this as evidence and further proof of Resurrection Day. The main concern of the Qur'ān is to improve the lifestyle of an individual through firm belief in the attributes of Allah and the Day of Resurrection.

> *Such is He Who knows all that is beyond the reach of a created being's perception, as well as all that can be witnessed by a creature's senses or mind: the Almighty, the Dispenser of Grace, Who makes excellent everything that He creates. And He begins the creation of man out of clay; then He causes him to be begotten out of the essence of a humble fluid; and then He forms him in accordance with what he is meant to be, and breathes into him of His spirit: and (these O people) He endows you with hearing, sight and insights: (yet) how seldom are you grateful.*
>
> (As-Sajdah, 32: 6–9)

Realities are divided into two categories – *ash-shahādah*, meaning that which is or can be witnessed and *al-ghayb*, meaning that which is beyond the reach of a created being's perception. Allah is the only One Who knows the reality of *al-ghayb*. This is the reason that He fashions every detail of His creation in accordance with the function intended for it, irrespective of whether those functions can be understood by us or are beyond the reach of our perceptions.

Allah, in declaring the 'beginning' of man's creation out of clay, denotes the basic composition of the body as such and He informs us about the pre-natal existence of each individual in the separate parental bodies. Allah's 'breathing of His Spirit into man' is a metaphor for the Divine gift of life and consciousness, or of a 'soul'.

The last stages of creation and procreation are the faculties of hearing, seeing, feeling and reasoning, boons which lead to a very meaningful life.

> *O Men! If you are in doubt as to the (truth of) Resurrection, (remember that) verily, We have created (every one of) you out of dust, then out of a drop of sperm, then out of a germ-cell, then out of an embryonic lump complete (in itself) and yet incomplete, so that We might make (your origin) clear unto you.*
>
> *And whatever We will (to be born) We cause to rest in the (mothers') wombs for a term set (by Us), and then We bring you forth as infants and (allow you to live) so that (some of) you might attain to maturity: for among you are such as are caused to die (in childhood), just as many a one of you is reduced in old age to a most abject state, ceasing to know anything of what he once knew so well.*
>
> *And (if, o man, you are still in doubt as to Resurrection, consider this): you can see the earth dry and lifeless –*

> *and (suddenly) when We send down waters upon it, it stirs and swells and puts forth every kind of lovely plant!*
>
> *All this (happens) because Allah alone is the Ultimate Truth, and because He has the power to will anything.*
>
> *And (know, o man) that the Last Hour is bound to come, beyond any doubt, and that Allah will (indeed) resurrect all who are in their graves.*
>
> (Al-Ḥajj, 22: 5–7)

The two types of embryonic lump (*muḍghah*) – 'complete in itself' (*mukhallaqah*) and 'yet incomplete' (*ghayr mukhallaqah*) – refer to the various stages of embryonic development. According to aṭ-Ṭabarī, *ghayr mukhallaqah* denotes the stage at which the *muḍghah* has yet no individual life, i.e. no soul has as yet been breathed into it.

The Qur'ān narrates the organic curve of a human's growth. The human being is reduced to a most abject state. The acquisition of bodily strength, intelligence and experience is followed by gradual decay and, in some cases, the utter helplessness of senility, comparable to the helplessness of a new-born child.

CHAPTER NINE

Initial Study of the Qur'ān

9.1 The Importance of Reading and Understanding the Qur'ān

Before studying the Qur'ān, the position of the student should be quite clear in relation to the Qur'ān. The Qur'ān is not an ordinary book from which every reader can benefit. It is a unique book, the only book in the world containing only the Words of Allah (God). Hence the primary principle of the Qur'ān must be known and grasped in order to benefit from its study.

This book is basically a guidebook for the Believers. A non-believer may read and may appreciate some points but it is not going to make a big impact on his/her lifestyle, if he/she is without a definite and clear opinion about the Qur'ān before undertaking any detailed study.

The reading and understanding of the Holy Qur'ān was emphasised by the Prophet (peace be upon him) and his Companions in many instances. Some of their exhortations are as follows:

(i) 'Uthmān (*ra*) reported that the Prophet (peace be upon him) remarked that whoever studies and teaches the Qur'ān is a better person (Bukhārī).

(ii) 'Ā'ishah (*ra*) narrated that the Prophet (peace be upon him) said that the expert in Qur'ānic studies will be amongst the company of the angels (Muslim).

(iii) 'Abdullāh ibn 'Umar (*ra*) reported that the Prophet (peace be upon him) reaffirmed that because of the blessings of the Qur'ān many people will be ahead of others (Muslim).

(iv) 'Umar ibn al-Khaṭṭāb (*ra*) confirmed that the Prophet (peace be upon him) instructed that all actions will be judged by their intentions. When reciting the Qur'ān make ablution and recite the Qur'ān in a clean place, concentrating on the fact that these are the Words of our Creator, Who is the Sustainer and Giver of life. Always start reading the Qur'ān by saying *Bismillāhir Raḥmānir Raḥīm,* meaning 'In the name of Allah, Most Gracious, Most Merciful'. When reading verses which give glad tidings and blessings, be happy, and those that provide warnings, cry or show fear. It is not correct to handle the *Muṣḥaf* (Qur'ān with Arabic version only) without ablution.

(v) Abū Ḥanīfah, the famous jurist mentioned that the reading of the Qur'ān should be finished in a minimum of 3 days. Whoever reads the complete Qur'ān twice a year has fulfilled his duties as the Prophet (peace be upon him) read the Qur'ān twice in the year he died.

(vi) 'Alī (*ra*) remarked that worship without anxiety, desire or question is incomplete.

(vii) Imām Ghazālī advised not completing any reading of the Qur'ān just so as to finish it. If one spends time reflecting on one verse it is better than spending the whole night reading the Qur'ān twice.

Many scholars have carried out a number of researches on all aspects of the Qur'ān, whether it be on medicine, astronomy, economics, law, technology, etc. Many others have spent a lifetime counting the number of vowels, dots, points, etc. employed in the Qur'ān. Other scholars have even counted the Arabic letters in the Holy Book.

9.2 Primary Principles About the Qur'ān

1. The Qur'ān is the direct Word of Allah that has reached the Believers through the Prophet (peace be upon him).
   (a) Its sanctity, inviolability and purity of text have to be accepted as a matter of fact.
   (b) The name Allah (*swt*) should not be taken lightly. It is the Supreme Name which has come to us through Revelation. It is the name that Allah (*swt*) has given to Himself.
   (c) Constant invocation of the Holy Name Allah (*swt*), contemplation of its characteristics and witnessing of its reverberations are essential to become fit for His light to descend into our soul.
   (d) The 'awareness' fostered by continual invocation of Allah (*swt*) and His other 99 names will accrue to the Believer's peace and tranquillity.
2. The Qur'ān, when recited, is heard by its Author Allah (*swt*). The Believer should always be conscious that he is reciting in the presence of Allah.
3. When the Believer meditates upon its contents in order to reach their true meaning, guidance is made available directly by Allah (*swt*) and He indeed cooperates with that person in their effort to reach the Truth.
4. The light which is radiated by the Divine Word has a transforming influence on the life of the Qur'ān reader. Just as sunshine affects the growth of plants, and is even

a pre-condition, so Allah Who is the Light of heaven and earth helps us to perceive the truth of our own situation inasmuch as He alone is our Maker and, therefore, fully aware of our needs, of our aspirations and of our limitations.

5. The Qur'ān emphasises the paramount need for the Believer to ask for forgiveness by reciting the numerous formulations of *Istighfār* (seeking forgiveness).

   And (always) seek Allah's forgiveness: behold, Allah is much-Forgiving, a Dispenser of Grace.

   (Al-Muzzammil, 73: 20)

   When Allah's succour comes, and victory, and you see people embrace Allah's religion in multitudes, extol your Sustainer's limitless glory, and praise Him, and seek His forgiveness. He is ever an acceptor of repentance.

   (An-Naṣr, 110: 1–3)

6. *Muḥkamāt* (clear without ambiguity) are the types of verses in the Qur'ān, the meaning of which is clear and admit no controversy.

   (a) The reader must abide by what these verses direct and by what they prohibit.

   (b) The reader should propagate this teaching in an attractive way firstly to his/her close relations and friends.

7. The verses which are *Mutashābihāt* (ambiguous) are cast in an analogical mould. Their meaning is not so easily decipherable.

   (a) The reader must try to meditate upon them and should also study the opinions of other learned authors of various commentaries.

   (b) The reader must not be loosely told about them at any stage or engage himself/herself in controversies about them.

8. The Qur'ān is a universal book. It is preserved in the guarded tablet (*lawḥ maḥfūẓ*) and the purity of its text has not been altered in the last 1400 years.

   Behold, it is We Ourselves Who have bestowed from on High, step by step, this reminder: and, behold, it is We Who shall truly guard it (from all corruption).

   (Al-Ḥijr, 15: 9)

9. As for the heart of a Believer, the Qur'ān is a source of his/her cure of his/her inward ailments, but upon one who is unjust (*ẓālim*), it has the effect of involving him/her in greater confusion, and in greater loss.

   Thus, step by step, We bestow from on High through this Qur'ān all that gives health (to the spirit) and is a grace unto those who believe (in Us), the while it only adds to the ruin of evil-doers.

   (Al-Isrā' 17: 82)

10. It is unsafe for the beginner to study the writings of non-believers about the Qur'ān.
11. The Book is the only miracle: Muḥammad (peace be upon him) was 'Qur'ān in action' as narrated by 'Ā'ishah (*ra*); that Muḥammad's (peace be upon him) conduct was moulded by the Qur'ān.

    When Our clear revelations are recited to them, those who do not hope to meet Us say to you: 'Bring us a Qur'ān other than this, or make changes in it.' Say: 'It is not for me to make a change in it by myself. I follow only what is revealed to me. I cannot disobey my Sustainer, for I fear the punishment of a fateful day.'

    (Yūnus 10: 15)

It was the miracle of the Qur'ān that gave to humanity the model of a man to illustrate its sublime morality. His sense of justice, and fair-play as even his love of all that was good and great in life are such that they have not been excelled by anyone.

> *All that is in heaven and earth glorifies Allah, the Sovereign Sustainer, the Holy One, the Almighty, the All-Knowing. It is He Who has sent forth among the unlettered a Messenger of their own to recite to them His revelations, to purify them, and to instruct them in the Scriptures and wisdom, things they have hitherto been in gross error.*
>
> (Al-Jumu'ah, 62: 1–2)

12. The historical role of the Prophet (peace be upon him) was to recite to the people Allah's Revelation.
13. The Prophet (peace be upon him) concludes the era of Revealed Religions. He is the last Prophet and no other Prophet will come after him to bring any new Revelation.
14. The historical mission of the Prophet (peace be upon him) represents a transitional phase. On the one hand, he concluded the era of Revealed Religion to mankind, and on the other, he laid the foundation for man to be able to actualise the truth of that Revelation by means of personal realisation.

9.3 Objectives of the Study

Every Believer has to act upon the teachings of the Qur'ān as well as invite others to understand and follow the Divine Guidance. These two tasks are quite different in approach hence this point must be thoroughly understood.

Study of the Qur'ān is an essential means by which to improve the quality of the Believers' lives and behaviour, individually as well as collectively. It basically relates to the Muslim community itself. Hence it is a community-oriented task. The Qur'ān in its compilatory order, is the guide for the

Muslim *Ummah*. Hence to work for the upgrading of the individual and the whole Muslim *Ummah*, study of the Qur'ān in its compilatory order is necessary.

The second task, of inviting others to Islam, is an obligation on all Believers. The study and presentation of the Qur'ān in this *da'wah* work or movement should be done with a different approach and methodology. For this task the Believers follow the *da'wah* approach and strategy of the Prophet Muḥammad (peace be upon him). He presented the verses of the Qur'ān to the non-believers in the same order as the Qur'ān was revealed to him. Hence, in this respect Muslims have to follow the sequence of Revelation and present it in the same order to non-believers.

This can perhaps best be understood by giving an example. The Qur'ān as thc compiled book after *Al-Fātiḥah* the abstract of the Book, talks about the history of past nations and Islamic laws. If these notions are presented to non-believers, they will not be very relevant. But if the explanation adopted follows the *sūrahs* in their order of revelation, i.e. the deeper concept of Allah (God), the life Hereafter and the mission of the Prophet (peace be upon him) is adopted, a non-believer may understand better what is being spoken about and may therefore take a greater interest in it.

9.4 Comprehension of the Qur'ān

What is the Qur'ān?

Without the Qur'ān, there is no authentic Islamic worldview and without the Prophet Muḥammad (peace be upon him) there is no perfect model of Islam. The Qur'ān deals with the three basic beliefs of Islam – the Oneness of Allah (*swt*), Life-after-Death and Divine Guidance. These three ideas are dealt with in the Qur'ān in different ways, in varying styles, and on different occasions – to make sure that a sincere reader becomes convinced. Divine Guidance cannot be followed without belief in the Supreme Lord and Master of the Universe and Life-after-Death in which rewards and punishments are given according to the accounts of the deeds performed in this world. Without reading and comprehending the Qur'ān, Islam can never be followed.

When and Where to Start

- Education and training begins in the cradle and ends with the grave. It is never too late to start.
- People who have embraced Islam at the age of 50, 60 or 70 years may well have started studying and comprehending the Qur'ān at that age. It is never too late.
- If you are worried about learning the Qur'ānic Arabic language, you may avoid it in the beginning. However, you should persist in your efforts to learn it.

The following are some easy sequential steps for those who cannot comprehend Qur'ānic Arabic.

1. Select a commentary on the Qur'ān in the language you understand best. For example, Mawdūdī and Iṣlāhī in Urdu, Sayyid Quṭb in Arabic, Ṭabaṭabā'ī in Persian, Nūrsī in Turkish, Pickthall, Abdullah Yusuf Ali and Hilali in English. A useful work on the Qur'ān for beginners is *The Qur'ān in Plain English* (Leicester, Islamic Foundation). Purchase and own the commentary and, if need be, make notes.
2. Commence from the beginning with the author's introduction. He will give you some hints and advice. Then start with the first and most important, *Sūrah al-Fātiḥah*. Read the Arabic text, the translation as compared with the Arabic text, and the explanations of the commentator.
3. Do not read more than half a page of the book at a time but be consistent in your reading every day after any Prayer. *Do not miss a day.* That is the proof of your interest. *No excuse in any way.*

4. Use a pencil to mark a tick (✓) for things you follow and understand, two ticks (✓✓) for things you do not know but are inspired by, a cross (x) for things that you do not comprehend, and a question mark (?) for things you do not understand.
5. After finishing one short *sūrah* or 5 pages of a long *sūrah* you should seek an appointment with a person who knows the Qur'ān to discuss with him/her, at least, the points that you have not understood.

9.5 The Qur'ān and *Ṣalāt*

Īmān (faith) and *'Amal al-Ṣāliḥ* (good deeds) are the two basic characteristics of Muslims. *Īmān* cannot be ingrained without comprehension of the Qur'ān and *'Amal al-Ṣāliḥ* can never be attained without the good performance of *ṣalāt.*

What is Ṣalāt?

- *Ṣalāt* is the communication between servants (ourselves) and the Master (Allah).
- *Ṣalāt* is to beg for all kinds of things from the Ultimate Giver of everything.
- *Ṣalāt* is to admit your mistakes to the Knower of all things and to ask forgiveness for small and large mistakes and sins committed between two *ṣalāt.* It is a secret of which only you and Allah are aware. There is no 'confession' in Islam. Hence you should not disclose your sins to anyone for atonement. You can take advice about these from someone in whom you have confidence.
- How can you talk to anyone especially to your Master if you do not know what you are saying? From a logical point of view it is ridiculous to offer *ṣalāt* without understanding the words that you are uttering.

Steps for a Meaningful Ṣalāt

1. Memorise *Sūrah* al-Fātiḥah and the last 10 *sūrahs* by heart with the proper punctuation and pronunciation together with the literal meaning of every word. This can be done within a month or two by those with a serious interest.
2. Get all this checked by someone who knows Arabic and is a devout Muslim with a thorough understanding of the Qur'ān.
3. Get a person competent in Arabic to check the words that you use in the five daily Prayers, for example, *sunnah, farḍ, nafl, witr.*
4. Get the translation of these words either from any standard Book of Prayer or from your Islamic teacher-friend. Memorise again the literal meaning of each and every word. This should take you not more than two months.
5. Have the whole Prayer checked every month by your teacher-friend, this for at least six months until you are confident and he/she approves. *Inshā' Allāh* your Prayers will now become meaningful and rewarding.

Glossary of Terms

Ākhirah: (After-Life, Hereafter, Next World). The term embraces the following ideas:

1. That man is answerable to God.
2. That the present order of existence will some day come to an end.
3. That when that happens, God will bring another order into being in which He will resurrect all human beings, gather them together and examine their conduct, and reward them with justice and mercy.
4. That those who are reckoned good will be sent to Paradise whereas the evil-doers will be consigned to Hell.
5. That the real measure of success or failure of a person is not the extent of his prosperity in the present life, but his success in the Next.

Āyah: A verse of the Qur'ān.

Da'wah: Invitation (to Islam).

Dīn: The core meaning of *dīn* is obedience. As a Qur'ānic technical term, *dīn* refers to the way of life and the system of conduct based on recognising God as one's sovereign and committing oneself to obey Him. According to Islam true *dīn* consists of living in total submission to God, and the way to do so is to accept as binding the guidance communicated through the Prophets.

Ḥajj (Major Pilgrimage) is one of the five pillars of Islam, a duty one must perform during one's life-time if one has the financial resources for it. It resembles *'Umrah* in some respects, but differs from it insofar as it can be performed only during certain specified dates of Dhū al-Ḥijjah. In addition to *ṭawāf* and *sa'y* (which are also required for *'Umrah*), there are a few other requirements but especially one's 'standing' (i.e. stay) in 'Arafāt during the day-time on 9th of Dhū al-Ḥijjah. For details of the rules of *Ḥajj*, see the books of *Fiqh*.

Hijrah signifies migration from a land where a Muslim is unable to live according to the precepts of his faith to a land where it is possible to do so. The *Hijrah par excellence* for Muslims is the *Hijrah* of the Prophet (peace be upon him) from the city of Makkah to Madinah which not only provided him and his followers refuge from persecution, but also an opportunity to build a society and state according to the ideals of Islam.

'Ibādah is used in three meanings: (1) worship and adoration; (2) obedience and submission; and (3) service and subjection. The fundamental message of Islam is that man, as God's creature, should direct his *'ibādah* to God in all the above-mentioned meanings of the term, and associate none with God in rendering it.

Iblīs literally means 'thoroughly disappointed; one in utter despair'. In Islamic terminology it denotes the *jinn*, who refused the command of God to prostrate before Adam out of vanity. He also asked God to allow him a term when he might mislead and tempt mankind to error. This term was granted to him by God whereafter he became the chief promoter of evil and prompted Adam and Eve to disobey God's order. He is also called *ash-Shayṭān* (Satan). He is possessed of a specific personality and is not just an abstract force.

Īmān: Faith, conviction.

Injīl signifies the inspired orations and utterances of Jesus (peace be upon him) which he delivered during the last two or three years of his earthly life in his capacity as a Prophet. The *Injīl* mentioned by the Qur'ān should, however, not be identified by the four Gospels of the New Testament which contain a great deal of material in addition to the inspired utterances of the Prophet Jesus (peace be upon him). Presumably the statements explicitly attributed to Jesus (peace be upon him) constitute parts of the true, original *Injīl.* It is significant, however, that the statements explicitly attributed to Jesus in the Gospels contain substantively the same teachings as those of the Qur'ān.

Jāhiliyyah literally, means 'ignorance'. It denotes all those world-views and ways of life which are based on rejection or disregard of heavenly guidance communicated to mankind through the Prophets and Messengers of God; the attitude of treating human life – either wholly or partly – as independent of the directives of God.

Jinn are an independent species of creation about which little is known except that unlike man, who was created out of earth, the *jinn* were created out of fire. But like man, a Divine Message has also been addressed to them and they too have been endowed with the capacity, again like man, to choose between good and evil, between obedience or disobedience to God.

Ka'bah: The House of Allah – focal point in Makkah towards which all Muslims turn for Prayer.

Kufr literally means 'to conceal'. This word has been variously used in the Qur'ān to denote: (1) state of absolute lack of faith; (2) rejection or denial of any of the essentials of Islam; (3) attitude of ingratitude and thanklessness to God; and (4) non-compliance with certain basic requirements of faith. In the accepted technical sense, *kufr* consists of rejection of the Divine Guidance communicated through the Prophets and Messengers of God. More specifically, ever since the advent of the last of the Prophets and Messengers, Muḥammad (peace be upon him), the rejection of his teachings constitutes *kufr.*

Ramaḍān: The Muslims' sacred month of fasting, the ninth month of the Muslim lunar calendar.

Risālah: The Prophethood, beginning with Adam and finalised by Muḥammad.

Ṣalāt literally means Prayer. In Islamic parlance *ṣalāt* refers to the ritual which is so-called because it includes praying.

Ṣalāt is an obligatory act of devotion which all adult Muslims are required to perform five times a day and consists of certain specific acts such as *takbīr* which signals the commencement of *ṣalāt*, and includes such other acts as *qiyām* (standing), *rukū'* (bowing), and *sujūd* (prostration).

Shirk consists of associating anyone or anything with the Creator either in His being, or attributes, or in the exclusive rights (such as worship) that He has against His creatures.

Sunnah: After the Qur'ān, the *Sunnah* is the most important source of the Islamic faith and refers essentially to the Prophet's example as indicated by his practise of the faith. The only way to know the *Sunnah* is through the collection of *aḥādīth* (the Traditions of the Prophet).

Tawḥīd: Unity – the basic concept of Islamic teaching – Oneness of Allah.

Ummah (literally 'collectivity', 'community', sharing the same origin or source) has been generally used in the Qur'ān to refer to all those who receive the Message of a Messenger of God, or happen to be living in an age when the teachings of that Messenger are extant.

Waqf, as a technical term, signifies the appropriation or dedication of property to charitable uses and to the service of God. It is an endowment the object of which must be of a perpetual nature so that the property so endowed may not be sold or transferred. Thus, while the substance of the property is retained, its usufruct is devoted to the good purposes laid down by its owner who, however, forfeits his power of its disposal, out of his intent to please God, by willing that his property be perpetually devoted to purposes that are pleasing to God.

Zakāt (Purifying Alms) literally means purification, whence it is used to express a portion of property bestowed in alms, as a means of purifying the person concerned and the remainder of his property. It is one of the five pillars of Islam and refers to the mandatory amount that a Muslim must pay out of his property. The detailed rules of *zakāt* have been laid down in books of *Fiqh*.

Index

'Abd al-Muṭṭalib, 89
'Abd ar-Raḥmān Jalāl-ad-Dīn as-Suyūṭī, 12
'Abdullāh ibn Mas'ūd, 101
'Abdullāh ibn 'Umar, 126
'Abdullāh ibn 'Umar al-Bayḍāwī, 12
Abdullāh Yusuf Ali, 132
Abraham, 24, 105
Abū Bakr Muḥammad, 118
Abū Bakr al-Ṣiddīq, 101
Abū Ḥanīfah, 126
Abū Ja'far Muḥammad ibn Jarīr aṭ-Ṭabari, 13
Abu'l A'lā Mawdūdī, Sayyid, 12, 132
Abu'l Faḍl Muḥammad Fakhruddīn ar-Rāzī, 12
Abu'l Faḍl Muḥammad ibn Mukarram ibn Manẓūr, 12
Abu'l Faraj al-Asfahānī, 116
Abu'l Fidā' Ismā'īl ibn Kathīr, 12
Abu'l Qāsim Ḥusayn ar-Rāghib, 12
Abu'l Qāsim al-Zahrāwī, 119
Abu'l Wafā', 118
Abū Mash'ar, 117
Abū Ṭālib, 89, 90
Abyssinia, 88
Adam, 16, 77, 78, 80, 82, 83, 84, 85, 96, 104, 105
Adultery, 73
Aḥad, 53, 55
'Ā'ishah, 126, 129
Ākhirah, 51, 67, 71
'Alī, 101, 126
'Alī ibn al-'Abbās, 119
Allah, *see* God
'Amal al-Ṣāliḥ, 133
Amīn Aḥsan Iṣlāḥī, 12, 132
Amman, 88
Andhra Pradesh, 24
Angels, 65, 77, 78, 79, 82, 83, 101, 126
Arabia, 24, 25, 45, 53, 59, 86, 87, 88, 89, 91
Arab(ic), 11, 17, 23, 25, 32, 112, 126, 127, 132
Arabs, 25, 53, 56, 87, 88, 99
Asia Minor, 60
'Aṣr Prayer, 66
Aṣ-Ṣamad, 55
Āyah, 42
Azerbaijan, 60

Babylon, 86
Badr, 60
Baghwad Gīta, 23
Banī Isrā'īl, 50, 79, 85, 112
Banū Hāshim, 89, 90
Basrah, 17
Al-Battanī, 118
Bible, the, 23, 31
Al-Bīrūnī, 116
Black Stone, 90
Bribery, 73
Buddhism, 103
Al-Bukhārī, 125
Byzantine(s), 59, 60

Capitalism, 103
Charity, 72

China, 86, 88
Christian era, 36
Christianity, 56, 98, 103
Christian(s), 59, 83, 86
Clorumia, 60
Communism, 103
Companions, 72, 101

Damascus, 116
David, 24, 105
Da'wah, 131
Day of Judgement, 72
Dīn, 33, 105, 106
Dumat al-Jandal, 88

Egypt, 85, 86, 88
England, 94
Europe, 45, 94
Eve, 80

Fajr Prayer, 66
Fasting, 72
Al-Fazarī, 117
Fu'ād, 109

Gambling, 73
George Bernard Shaw, 94
Al-Ghazālī, 126
Gifts, 72
God, 7, 8, 9, 10, 11, 13, 15, 17, 18, 19, 21, 23, 24, 25, 26, 27, 28, 30, 33, 36, 38, 39, 41, 43, 46, 49, 50, 51, 53, 54, 55, 56, 57, 58, 59, 60, 64, 65, 66, 67, 68, 69, 70, 71, 72, 76, 77, 78, 79, 80, 81, 82, 83, 84, 85, 86, 87, 89, 91, 92, 93, 95, 96, 97, 98, 101, 103, 104, 105, 107, 108, 109, 110, 111, 112, 113, 122, 123, 125, 126, 127, 128, 130, 132, 133
Goethe, 94
Gospels, the, 24, 47
Greece, 31, 86, 120

Habashah (Abyssinia), 59
Ḥajj, 8, 73
Ḥamīduddīn Farāhī, 12
Hell, 63, 72
Heraclius, 60
Hereafter, 29, 46, 60, 61, 62, 63, 64, 65, 104, 131
Hijrah, 59
Hilali, 132
Ḥilf al-Fuḍūl, 89, 90
Hindu(s), 7, 98, 103
Hyderabad, 24

'Ibādah, 84
Iblīs, 78, 82, 83, 84
Ibn 'Asākir, 116
Ibn Baṭṭūṭah, 115
Ibn al-Bayṭār, 119
Ibn al-Ḥaithām, 119
Ibn Ḥayyān, 116
Ibn Khaldūn, 116
Ibn al-Khatīb, 120
Ibn Rushd, 120
Ibn Sīnā, 120
Ibn Zuhr, 120
Ibrāhīm, 85, 88
Al-Idrīsī, 116
Īmān, 133
India, 7, 24, 86, 88
Injīl, 32
Iran, 60, 88
'Īsā, 85
Isaac, 112
Isḥāq, 112
Islam(ic), 7, 8, 9, 14, 17, 20, 23, 26, 33, 45, 51, 53, 55, 66, 71, 72, 94, 96, 99, 103, 104, 106, 107, 111, 112, 113, 131
Ismā'īl, 85
Israelites, 85
Issus, 60
Al-Iṣṭakhrī, 116

Jābir ibn Ḥayyān, 118
Jacob, 112
Jāhiliyyah, 20
Al-Jāḥiẓ, 119
Jeddah, 88
Jesus, 24, 31, 85, 86, 96, 105
Jews, 85, 86
Jinn, 78, 82, 83
Jordan, 59
Judaism, 103

Ka'bah, 73, 85, 86, 90, 95
Khadījah, 91, 92
Khalīfah, 76
Al-Khaṭīb al-Baghdādī, 116
Al-Khawārizmī, 116, 117
Kufah, 17
Kufr, 50
Kuttāb al-Waḥy, 101

Last Day, 78
Life-after-Death, 46, 68, 96, 103, 131, 132
Loans, 72

Madinah, 17, 51, 59, 60
Maghrib Prayer, 66
Maḥmūd ibn 'Umar az-Zamakhsharī, 12
Makkah, 17, 51, 60, 85, 86, 88, 89, 90, 91, 94, 101
Martyrs, 65
Al-Mas'ūdī, 115
Minhāj, 33
Moses, 24, 27, 96, 105
Mount Ḥirā', 91, 92
Muḥammad ibn 'Alī Ash-Shawkānī, 12
Muḥammad, the Prophet, 8, 9, 10, 13, 23, 24, 25, 26, 29, 30, 31, 33, 36, 37, 38, 42, 43, 46, 51, 53, 55, 59, 60, 66, 71, 72, 85, 86, 87, 89, 90, 91, 92, 93, 94, 95, 96, 98, 99, 101, 104, 111, 112, 125, 126, 129, 130
Muḥammad Rashīd Riḍā, 12
Al-Muqaddasī, 116
Murtaḍā az-Zabīdī, 12
Mūsā, 85
Mūsā ibn Shākir, 117
Muṣḥaf, 13, 102, 126
Muslim, 126
Muslim(s), 7, 8, 9, 10, 11, 14, 16, 20, 24, 60, 95, 96, 100, 101, 105, 110, 115, 133

Natural Sciences, 115
Next Life, 29, 71
Next World, 20, 51
Nūḥ, 88
Nūrsī, 132

Orientalists, 24
Osmania University, 24
Other World, 103

Pagans, 86
Palestine, 59
Paradise, 29, 66, 72, 80
Persia(ns), 59, 60, 86, 88, 132
Pharaoh, 85
Pickthall, 132
Polytheists, 53, 55, 60, 65
Prayer(s), 66, 72, 73, 91, 134
Property, 73
Prophets, 24, 27, 31, 33, 47, 48, 50, 64, 65, 84, 85, 88, 96, 98, 104, 105
Psalms, the, 24, 47

Qur'ān, the, 7, 8, 9, 10, 11, 12, 13, 15, 17, 19, 21, 23, 24, 25, 26, 27, 28, 29, 30, 31, 32, 33, 35, 36, 37, 38, 39, 40, 41, 42, 43, 45, 46, 47, 48, 49, 50, 51, 56, 60, 63, 66, 71, 72, 76, 83, 85, 86, 88, 91, 94, 96, 97, 98, 99, 100, 101, 102, 104, 105, 106, 108, 109, 110, 111, 113, 115, 120, 121, 124, 125, 126, 127, 128, 129, 132, 133, 134

Quraysh, 17, 56, 60, 86, 88, 89, 90
Quṭb, Sayyid, 12, 132

Ramaḍān, 101
Ar-Rāzī, 118, 119
Renaissance, the, 45
Resurrection Day, 65, 66, 71, 122
Risālah, 51
Romans, 59, 60
Rome, 86, 88

Saint(s), 65, 93
Ṣalāt, 133, 134
Sanaa, 88
Satan, 65, 78, 80, 82, 83, 84
Science, 120, 122
Scrolls, the, 24
Sharī'ah, 33
Shirk, 50, 65
Socialism, 103
Spain, 116
Sunnah, 8, 15, 99, 100, 134
Syria, 17, 59

Aṭ-Ṭabarī, 115, 124
Ṭabaṭabā'ī, 132
Ṭā'if, 86

Taurus Mountains, 60
Tawḥīd, 51, 56, 57, 67, 71, 105
Torah, the, 23, 24, 47
Turkey, 132

'Umar al-Khayyām, 118
'Umar ibn al-Khaṭṭāb, 101, 126
Ummah, 8, 10, 79, 104, 112, 131
Ur, 88
Urdu, 132
Usury, 86
'Uthmān, 101, 102, 125

Waqf, 72
Wills, 72

Yaḥyā ibn Māsawayah, 119
Yamamah, 101
Yanbu', 88
Ya'qūb, 112
Yāqūt ar-Rūmī, 117
Yemen, 88, 90

Zakāt, 72
Az-Zarqall, 117
Zayd ibn Thābit, 101
Zoroaster, 60
Ẓuhr Prayer, 66